PRAISE FOR ARIC H. MORRISON

Aric once again takes his readers on the ride of unpredictability in a way not many can do. Holy cow, the ending was a shocker!

— VICTORIA REAGAN, PUBLICIST, SAN FRANSICO, CA.

Aric H. Morrison may have written one of any book's most disturbingly surreal moments. The last chapter.

— THE BOOKMARK

The writing deserves a standing ovation. Incredible storytelling. Knowing this is all true makes it even more impactful.

— TC PUBLISHING

I am glad to breathe again. The next book in the series cannot come soon enough!

Bravo Aric!

— SUSAN DUDEK, ANAPOLIS, M.D

TRACING RAINDROPS

TRACING RAINDROPS

ABOVE THE CLOUDS, THE SUN STILL SHINES

ARIC H. MORRISON

THIRSTY CAMEL
PUBLISHING

TRACING RAINDROPS - An Inspirational True Story

Above The Clouds, The Sun Still Shines

Aric H. Morrison

Published by:

Thirsty Camel Publishing

2nd Edition 4/14/25

ISBN: 978-1-958246-32-0

Library of Congress Control Number: 2025906710

1st Edition Published 8/2/23

This book is thoughtfully dedicated to those who like me, still wish for impossible things.

Aric H. Morrison is a huge fan of my brother Eric Carr of the Hall of Fame rock band KISS. Over the years, I have gotten to know him as a friend; he is a very unselfish soul.

Bless You, Aric!

— LORETTA CARAVELLO - (ERIC'S SISTER)

EPIGRAPH

"Even in your next failure, you are admired by someone else who hasn't reached that height yet."

— ARIC H. MORRISON

FOREWORD

The second installment of *The Stealing Home Series*, *Tracing Raindrops* by Aric H. Morrison, continues with the trials and tribulations of the unknown when dealing with adversity tied to life—a deeply moving, emotional, unchartered time, as experienced by the Morrison Family.

My career has spanned over 30 years in the Retail Gas Station and Convenience Store business. It's a great industry! I have worked and shared rewarding yet stressful times with tremendous employees, friends, customers, suppliers, and executives throughout the United States.

In my capacity, there are very few life exposures that are unfamiliar. Experiential learning has always influenced me to do what is right for the employee, their family, and the company.

I was by far put to the test via Aric's remarkable journey. Not for lack of support from me but due to the seemingly constant barrage of adversities that had singled him out for some reason. It is safe to say, "My number one priority quickly became the need to support The Morrison Family."

Aric and I have known each other professionally for over 20 years as co-workers, but more so now as lifelong friends. I first met him in Pennsylvania when he accepted a role to lead a market acquisition. On day one, he was dressed sharply in shiny shoes, a new suit, a debonair tie, and ready to tackle the world. This new guy from NH was prepared to conquer!

It was a memorable day for both of us; I gently broke the news we stopped wearing suits and ties to work over a year ago. Sharing a good laugh set the tone for how we would be after that!

For a man with such an incredibly infectious sense of humor, there was always a guardedness about his past. Until reading *Heavenly Peace*, I hadn't known much of it.

I remember when Stacey and Aric announced they were expecting their second child. Everyone was thrilled as the family was doing well, and he was thriving in his new role! Not once had I been made aware of the darker mortality struggle behind the scenes presented in this book until I read it.

Aric H. wears a highly complex mask.

Since meeting him, medical trauma, family support, roles, and life balance have different meanings for me. What strikes me is how positively he presented himself when speaking about his family. Until now, remaining humble, most of his story has never been told.

I was on a plane while reading the first one in *The Stealing Home Series*. I never put the book down! Aric has been talking about writing these almost for as long as I have known him.

Without a doubt, he delivered in his pursuit.

The main body of this story was as foreign to me as much of the first one. Aside from having met his entire family, I, too, was incredulous while reading it.

This family always had the full support of our corporation personally and professionally, yet we only knew about half of what was going on. Unique to his ability to minimize the harsh truth, these details remained under wraps.

No matter the challenge, Aric could still find the balance between his family and dedication to work. His passion for them was unbelievable while remaining highly focused on guiding his team to success as a business unit. He provided leadership versatility, empowered others, and achieved key metrics for his business unit consecutively for years. Coincidentally, he made it all happen simultaneously with events in this series.

If this is not the epitome of an Adversity Rockstar®, I would be unable to define one otherwise.

Tracing Raindrops will certainly not disappoint. When the subject is so personal, Aric's way of sharing guides the reader very quickly into his mind. The story flows so brilliantly; he never allows that person to leave it!

The ending was brutal because I recall my conversation with him one day later. I, too, have struggled with it.

To conclude, few breaks have come his way as Aric H. has been sucker-punched incessantly. One man should never be faced with the dealings associated with such an unfair life.

However, it doesn't surprise me to learn of his incredible success as an authority figure on adversity and as an Inspirational Speaker and Award-Winning Author touring the country in both capacities.

His time has come. This guy can write and tell one heck of a story.

Hopefully, he has since ditched that suit by now!

Paul Brzezicki
Retired - Sales and Operations Executive
Highly Visible, Accessible, and Transformational Leader
Sunoco LP
Hess Corporation
Dallas, Texas

PREFACE

As I have mentioned, a lot is left undone in reconciling what happened when I was a kid. Almost every day, I still suffer from other continuously scarring flashbacks as I share more emotionally painful details throughout this series and on stage when referencing some of this.

Screaming whispers refer to these darker shadows from my past. I coined this simple term a bit ago, which felt more than appropriate to represent them. The contrast between the two words makes sense as you consider it.

They are composed of those angst ridden memories unwilling to allow healing from their painful influences. Some dim a little, but many never disappear and are destined to remain. They can haunt you at the most inopportune time and even suddenly cause your eyes to open from a sound sleep.

When you place every one of these random images into one disintegrating mind such as mine, it becomes a real haunting shit show.

They routinely take turns knifing me in the brain. To this day, they are ever present, though I wish them never to surface again. Unfortunately, the more colorless the image, the heavier it tends to weigh. Is it my form of escapism reflecting so much, or is it a curse because the bad contained there also lurks in my cranial shadows?

I don't know the answer.

The tricky part of being this age now is trying to sift through those challenging periods to process them properly. I can better accept some for what they were, while most will take longer. Many of these torment me in ways no human should have to experience. Ever.

Death is a conceptual reality that has sidled next to me throughout my entire life, too. I mentioned it numerous times in the first installment, as it remained just one step behind me during this phase. This, by far, is my most complex psychological issue.

My family had more downs than ups, much different than most others. As you will read, ours became an outlier to the ways we are *supposed* to be. Instead, my perfect vision of happiness slowly turned into something else.

My emotional trek continues here; read through this mix of high and low shadow-filled innings while I share them with you as joyfully and achingly as they occurred.

This is *Tracing Raindrops.*

TRACING RAINDROPS
ABOVE THE CLOUDS, THE SUN STILL SHINES

GAME TWO

* * *

PREGAME

AHEAD

Simple times allowed for simple solutions when we were innocent. Isn't it funny when we are young, there is a belief that if we block out the bad and scary stuff around us, doing so will magically make it all disappear?

It is almost as if we figuratively closed our eyes tightly, counted to ten, and then expected when we reopened them to be all well with the world again.

When you have less than a decade of life experience, the easiest solution to your troubles can be to run away and hide. Magically, time assumes a new role and those around us who have caused the anxiety again become approachable.

Suppose it were only that easy. As adults, we experience reality kicking us in the teeth. Burying our heads will only deposit a lot of sand in our ears and hair. It solves nothing by avoiding that which troubles us.

We learn to march ahead and deal with what we are given, whether we like it or not. No one ever said this journey would be easy.

There was no choice but to face reality back in 2006 when we were told that our unborn child would eventually be lost due to a miscarriage. We weren't about to pretend, cower, or massage their words, though we may have wanted to on more than one occasion. It all happened so fast that day in February, as though a movie crew had come into our lives and placed us on some strange new set with an unrehearsed plot twist for us to rehearse repeatedly.

As you may recall, in the first book, Stacy and I drove home to share the news with Aryn after hearing the unfortunate information regarding the ruptured placenta. The sound of car doors slamming that cold day echoed through the trees around our home in Peterborough, causing snow to jump from a few branches and cascade down to the lawn. Everything else was quiet and still as we walked up our granite front steps in disbelief.

We were both processing how bleak the outlook was for our baby and needed additional time to gather ourselves, so we put off having that terrible conversation with him regarding his brother. If she and I were not in the right frame of mind, how could we do the conversation any justice?

The odds for repair and recovery were slim, but nothing was ever one hundred percent final, either. *Screw the previous diagnosis,* we felt after a couple of days. Instead, we rocked along as a family to make it as far as we had; our mission was always to prove that there is more to the human spirit than most people are in tune with.

In fairness, since they said we had a chance for our son to be born, we did our best to bottle up whatever positive energies were available and used them to our advantage.

There was never any buried-head-in-the-sand nonsense going on with us. We hadn't done that through Aryn's medical crisis, nor were we about to begin doing so with this baby. We moved ahead and planned accordingly to become parents to another boy. Period.

What else would anyone do in this scenario? Sit around and wait for something terrible to happen. We weren't unfamiliar with facing headwinds. Here was another one.

In honesty, Stacey and I had not discussed fluid loss or losing the baby in detail after those first few long days, save for our initial plans to set them both up to have a decent chance of beating those odds.

We believed in forcing God's hand, knowing he was making a mistake in trying to take our child from us.

Via a makeshift triage at home, Stacey remained on complete bed rest indefinitely. As the doctors had instructed, she needed to stay horizontal for any possible reversals of her current placenta situation. This meant modifying every aspect of our usual way of conducting family business. When you have a five-year-old boy around the house, forcing oneself not to be vertical becomes challenging.

You could almost say we altered our lifestyle to invest in *possibility* rather than bow down to *definitive*. It was a strange way to consider it, but there we were.

Together, we rallied every day, hoping to get us that much closer to our due date in July. Rather than thinking about how much the shift impacted us, we marched along, trying to keep strong. In many respects, it is all a blur of how quickly we took control of amending our lives. The days of running to the store or pharmacy, picking up Aryn at school, or simply heading into town for a warm meal became a thing of the past.

I maintained my hectic work schedule during the weekdays and took over around the house on the weekend, picking up the slack from Stacey, who was not able to do as much as she was accustomed to. I also tried to be more influential in keeping our days positive and hopeful.

We made it work.

Like everything else traumatic, when you walk through complicated days, the sense of urgency dissipates as time progresses. Taking stock each morning to convince ourselves silently everything would be okay was as common as showering. We never acknowledged any self-repairing progress as it happened within, but we knew our efforts were difference-makers in the long run.

Maybe we just got tired of worrying, but gradually, there seemed to be a more positive shift or substantial presence building within us. Our little guy never indicated that he would allow any adverse opportunity to overtake his life plan to survive, either. We were then back to being mission-focused in a routine pregnancy way.

His advancement for the rest of March 2006 seemed to minimize any immediate risks of miscarriage, as they eventually became smaller and smaller. Incredibly, the heart was still beating very strongly and had never weakened during this craziness.

As Stacey felt better and the weeks chugged along, maybe we self-ishly began to judge, based on his resilience thus far, that all would be okay. Whatever it was to help change the plans for destiny, it worked. The unthinkable never presented itself in any way.

Unquestionably, our unborn son, who was supposed to have passed, was doing everything he could to survive, fighting to become a part of our family. He was trying to prove he was destined to join us.

This is wild to read; I get it. Knowing what I now know about how this story unfolded, it's the only conclusion I would draw today.

Was it her persistence to stay off her feet or his inner spirit that may have saved this baby and preserved his birth?

Was it our commitment to staying positive, or was it his strong will to fight and meet his family?

Was it both of their souls joining forces to prove once and for all that miracles do happen?

Whether we wanted to attribute this to hope, faith or divine inter-vention made no difference. We knew that our sheer scale of skep-ticism to optimism had started to tilt.

Toward the end of the month, it became as though that terrible day a month and a half back in February had never even been real. Eventually, accepting that our son was defying the odds of medical science, we proceeded. We knew there would still be a long, uneasy stretch ahead of us, but not in such a consequential way anymore.

He wasn't giving up.

Nor were we.

When the Boston Red Sox took the field for their first home opener of the year against the Toronto Blue Jays on April 7, 2006, we were very optimistic that things were on pace to turn out positively regarding this pregnancy.

It might have been nice to write so early on in this story that Stacey and I were ultimately headed toward a warm and fuzzy place where the puffy clouds above looked like cotton candy and the warm spring breeze smelled of freshly baked apple pie, thanks to our unconventional efforts.

It sure would have been lovely, but where our story continues here took us in an entirely new direction. Where we were headed was quite the opposite.

Welcome back.

FIRST INNING

* * *

SIP

It is convenient to plop on a comfy couch each morning, bang away at my keys, sit on my drum throne at night, and bang away at the skins. Both provide the same comfort to me and are instant in their reciprocation. I use them semi-equally to breathe, practice grounding, and reset.

It rarely works. I am too damaged from the last 24 years. The next portion of this difficult era began in this first grouping of innings.

This book has taken me a long time to finish because, directionally, it might have gone several different ways. I could have easily carried my readers to a horrible place the way it was inside for me. Depression and anxiety are a lifelong poison of mine. The entire *Stealing Home Series* is bound together by their attributes in one way and cathartically healing in another.

I decided that how I share much of this one needed to remain somewhere in the middle range of white to black. It was the best for now. The next one will certainly not disappoint if the darkness appeals to you. Know that I was trying hard to maintain a healthy work-life balance, remain supportive towards my wife, and be a great dad to Aryn.

What I neglected was never taking the time to address my internal emotional wrangling. It was a huge mistake. Like a snowball rolling down a hill, my demons kept gathering more and more momentum.

There is always, always, always a steady supply of reflective material flowing through these authorship veins, keeping the rest of me fully charged and ready to go. With it comes a ton of regrets and frustrations.

Lately, so much time at my disposal has uniquely worked into a daily routine. With each freshly brewed cup of morning caffeine comes an incredible array of sentiments. It is almost as though one may not exist without the other. I need my coffee, but the tan and teal-colored, round, big-loop-handled cup rarely kisses my lips without becoming a thought trigger.

It's on first thing, and then later in the day, it *is on* again as quickly as another refill is welcomed in my empty mug. Fateful thoughts regularly break free from the chaos in this heavily trafficked racing skull.

Freedom to ponder has allowed most of the trauma to remain sharply in my head. Writing this series has repeatedly reminded me to stop and compartmentalize who I am. This inability to understand my position in life seems to be on my mind the most. Should I be content with where my five-decade journey has brought me? Have I been fighting for something not meant for me and never realized it until now?

Did **Fate** have this confused mess planned for me from birth?

I will never know these answers, but this ongoing flow of contemplation is how it seems. There is certainly no shortage of time to consider where I fit in all this human stuff. It is a massive concept to toss out there, but I wonder how many people do this.

I speak about life being a series of images and flashbacks; we recall them as frequently or infrequently as we choose. The more painful ones in mine remain vivid and clear.

For me, the bad stuff never seems to fade in the least, while the better days need to be coaxed back out. It is almost as though this sort of counterbalance is by design.

Are we all supposed to pause regularly and think about our existence? And then, do we live with regret if reality doesn't match our dreams?

Is it time to ponder what we have seen, accomplished, shared, endured, or, in my case, have been blessed/cursed to experience in this journey?

At the very least, are we faithful in our pursuit of being who we were meant to become?

I'm half a century old; the last 24 years have definitely taken their toll. At times, I feel unfulfilled and unprosperous because of my years. The next day, I petition for positivity. I want more out of life and more out of the time left here, and I strive for more opportunities to start over again.

It will never happen.

Instead, I can only use whatever quantity the hourglass has left in it to share this bumpy ride with you.

When you ask yourself what your most significant accomplishment (aside from having children) is, does an answer come instantly to you?

Perhaps if we all performed this exercise on our birthdays at the beginning of the new decade, our perspectives would differ every ten years.

Maybe it is meant to be.

Do we find ourselves living the life we are in because of our decisions and not of some grand master plan at all?

Maybe there isn't one.

After many long sit-downs with Fate, the same question has been posed repeatedly: "Why?"

I'm still waiting for the answer.

APART

TUESDAY, MAY 2, 2006

A rapid, life-altering progression occurred over the first four days of May, which sped toward us with minimal advanced warning. As usual, we were, once again, entirely caught off guard.

The beginning of our next phase.

Stacey and I awoke at the usual time on this beautiful spring morning. Due to our circumstances with that placenta mess, every day was planned out systematically and carefully. If routine and caution were written across our foreheads, they were synonymous with us.

We got Aryn ready for school and continued to make plans for the evening. Like every other day before this one, we performed the same morning routine with one exception: Stacey was headed down to Boston for a consult at one of those medical facilities just down the road from Fenway Park.

Today was the introductory visit to discuss where our hard work to keep her horizontal had taken us. Due to the delicate nature of our pregnancy, she was referred to this facility for the remaining months of this term. In some respects, it was nice to be seen by this vast new entity. But doing so also highlighted how serious our situation still was.

Not having been to Brigham and Women's Hospital before this visit, it was awkward for her to navigate various routes, exits, and ramps in and around the city without using a GPS device. Over time, it makes sense, but initially, it is hard without practice. Eventually, things will look familiar if you get lost enough there.

After arriving by mid-morning, the schedule consisted of complex testing so they could get a complete detailed understanding of how to proceed with such a precarious pregnancy. And so they began.

Initially, the experience was strangely familiar, as there was mention of the same repetitive concerns we had already heard about with Aryn five years earlier.

This particular day, I was traveling in and around the Boston area on business, but I hadn't planned on spending any time at the hospital with Stacey. It was supposed to be just another check-up like the others that had taken place before, and there was no apparent need for me to be there.

In addition to the tests, they planned on monitoring the baby extensively and mapping out a plan for the remaining three months of the pregnancy. Why bother going?

I spoke with her twice later in the morning, and she confirmed that they spent much time examining his size, including bone structure and organ development. It was all pretty standard stuff for a first visit.

Not much information was returned besides the affirmation that our son was extremely tiny. We already knew that. Where was the breakthrough here?

Because his momma had been on bed rest for so long, I was in the routine of driving home from NH, MA, or RI most days to do the honors of picking my son up. He didn't ride a bus; instead, Aryn attended a daycare program with many friends for a few hours after elementary school let out.

Watching him get excited when I arrived made all the crazy adjusted scheduling worth it—a fantastic way to allow my business side to remain at bay temporarily until the next day.

Stacey had packed an overnight bag, as we knew she would be monitored throughout the evening there in Boston. The test results scheduled to return in the morning were supposed to shed more light on things, so the inconvenience of staying there was worth the effort. Funnily, she had a night all to herself.

After explaining that his mommy was at the hospital and the doctors were checking on his brother, Aryn shrugged and brushed it off. He was used to us talking about the many trips we made to medical places, so truthfully, this conversation was relatively routine for him. He was so young then, too; there wasn't much to worry about in terms of profoundly processing what was happening. It was all surface stuff barely skimming his mind.

"Did someone buy the Cheese-its?"

Aryn didn't display any genuine concern one way or another while eating his nachos with cheese at a favorite restaurant in Peterborough called Brady's. Tonight was one of the first few evenings his mother wasn't sleeping at home with us, so this provided a new twist regarding our after-dinner dynamic, in a father-son kind of way. We enjoyed some bonding while stuffing our faces with unhealthy food over a few silly laughs.

The evening continued with the same structure as always. A typical one included bath time and cartoons before bed. He liked having a bite to eat with his milk during TV time, and we served his snacks on paper plates shaped like animals. To make a child smile, an elephant or lion's face looking back at them is simple. This is what you do as a parent—create happiness.

He always enjoyed seeing what animal was on it, and we pretended quite regularly that when we took an item off the plate to eat it, we were also consuming a small part of the zoo creature.

Stacey called home around seven for one final check-in and gave me an update on what the next day had in store for us. She appeared to be taking it all in stride even though she was alone in the hospital with no company. I assured her Aryn would receive a kiss goodnight on her behalf and confirmed my being there in the morning for the consults with the physicians.

Typically, we read two books of his choosing. Then, his mom and I remained in bed next to him for a short time. He usually fell sound asleep within ten to fifteen minutes. From there, it was adult time to decompress, relax, and prepare for the next day.

Tonight, as we all were about to, Aryn slept without a worry on his mind.

Upon hearing his heavy breathing and waiting a few minutes to be sure he was asleep, I gently leaned over, kissed his cheek, and whispered as I always did.

"Goodnight; Daddy loves you and will always be with you."

I believed these words were appropriate to say each night to him just in case I was later taken in my sleep. After experiencing my father's passing suddenly in 1988, this reassurance was my way of forcing minor closure.

You never know.

Today, I'd give anything to return in time just once to relive a typical night full of rituals like those we shared. It was calculated but so pure and a delicate part of his upbringing. I guess that is why specific memories are so important. At the very least, they can conjure a quick smile if needed.

Like so much in life, we don't appreciate the little things until later on down the road.

RIDE

WEDNESDAY, MAY 3, 2006

I guess, in some way, what we had done by keeping Stacey off her feet made it possible for us even to be where we were. But it was of little consequence in the big picture now. Here, we thought our efforts were making a difference, only to learn that his situation was much more severe than anyone had determined previously.

Today, we were about to discover that we had a real mess on our hands after being only six months along. This pregnancy was super complex, with another dramatic set of entanglements marching our way.

Just like that, the Morrison family shit was once again ready to hit the fan.

I followed the routine of preparing Aryn and myself to rock and roll. The schedule was to drop him off at school, go to work in Boston and meet Stacey with the doctors, drive back, pick him up, and begin the evening duties while waiting for her to come home later. Bing, bang, boom, all in a day's work.

Aside from her complaints about the catheter placed earlier in the morning, she was in good spirits and propped up on her hospital bed to the room's right. Blood was drawn regularly the previous evening, so understandably, my wife was exhausted and worn out.

I was glad to be there as we both anticipated new directions and professional guidance. Feeling like the worst days were behind us, remaining a day or two in the hospital felt like nothing. Overall, we were both pretty upbeat—lots of smiling and small talk.

We moved into a conference room with five or six medical professionals. For the first of many scheduled meetings, each lasting about thirty to forty-five minutes, we began a long and deliberate information-sharing process.

Surprisingly, there was no mention of the placenta stuff; today, it was all about his lack of development and current size. I wondered if he lost some growth time during the scare but never got a definitive answer, as we quickly learned it made no difference.

There was much more going on—or not.

We became very attentive while eventually accepting that our son was in serious trouble. He had been for quite some time.

The conversation moved along slowly, like a case of the same script, a different child all over again. What we were being told was eerily parallel to the discussion before Aryn was born, when Stacey and I sat side by side in silence, listening to another series of complicated and unsettling scenarios. This time, it was much more complex.

Unfortunately, I had a few bad flashbacks during each of these conversations, which revved up my anxiety after the meeting. It hadn't taken long to realize this pregnancy wasn't what we may have thought it to have been. There has been almost no progress made by our efforts.

He, too, had attached to one side of the womb and was ultimately not gaining the full range of space. Whereas the baby's development had been slow but gradual in those first three months, it wasn't the case anymore. Now, there was none.

This stark reality that our son had not developed for quite some time was a huge concern for everyone. If not by their faces, certainly by the tone of voices, everyone we met with was of the same demeanor. This was some complicated stuff.

Very few options came our way shortly after being made aware of this, so this sudden rush of information seemed to leave us confused about where we were headed next.

How the heck did this pregnancy get back on track?

Unthinkingly, we could hold steady the current course and pray for conditions to improve, hoping for the nearly impossible. We'd be placing a false belief in the potential that our baby would suddenly be able to somehow grow again for three more months in the same environment and be delivered as scheduled the last week in July.

Since the baby was already restricted, how would it even happen? For this process to work flawlessly, we also needed to assume that the organs would start developing independently. Everything in this do-nothing-but-wait-and-see scenario went against medical facts and case history.

(We knew almost instantly *that ship* had sailed.) In actuality, it was out of the question.

We would have been fooling ourselves here as the doctors didn't even attempt to sell us on this one. It was a fantasy tale leading to an awful outcome, almost guaranteed.

Some steps needed to be taken, but what the heck was the right thing to do?

If they were going to try and save his life by delivering him prematurely, taken by c-section like Aryn, the probability of being born with significant complications and life-altering restrictions was astronomically high. This baby was three months early and had already been behind substantially due to Stacey's abnormal womb limitations.

This all, of course, was contingent upon his ability even to make it through the delivery.

What a dilemma.

DRIP

I ronically, within a mile, happy families rushed carefree around Fenway while we sat in a medical row, suddenly blindsided. There is no picnic in the park when you are in complex meetings for hours to discuss probabilities as they pertain to those that you possess minimal control over influencing.

The roads around the ballpark were crammed with fans seeking to check off a few bucket list items as the Toronto Blue Jays were again in town. Revelers surrounded the area reasonably early on the day of any Sox game. To make matters worse, I had to drive through it all on my way home.

These days, there was electricity in the air all around that part of Boston, creeping over to the vicinity where we were. Many folks parked in the hospital garages and walked on over from there to get to Fenway. Two contrasting worlds were set in motion, hence my fascination with this irony—a high and a low point co-existing just down the road.

It is not uncommon to even see fans in those hospital lobbies wearing their Sox clothing while grabbing a coffee or just coming inside to cool off in the air conditioning.

Depending on their situation, the masses were even known to work half days and then enjoy preparing for the game by imbibing at the various drinking venues around the Back Bay and Copley areas. I have been there and done that many times. (Easy to do when you don't have a crap ton of question marks circling above your head.)

Today might have been a nice getaway, too, but obviously, we had more important things to deal with than a foamy head on the top of a cold glass with an order of crispy fries on the side. The highs and lows of unpredictability were in full motion for Stacey and me.

Though my love for the team, the sport, and the ballpark has never subsided, watching baseball was the furthest thing from my mind. This much fun would amount to a kick in the balls after the times we were having.

In reality, we were facing a lose-lose set of scenarios and odds that seemed to be getting more intense by the minute. Just outside the window, fans were rushing north toward Fenway. Both worlds collided in front of me that day.

It was fitting.

No one at the hospital could state definitively to what extent the organs had formed, but they all repeated emphatically that his heart, lungs, and other vitals were utterly underdeveloped. And they were too small to support life independently outside the womb based on his current status today.

This much was certain.

Incredibly, after the third hour, they introduced the concept of administering powerful steroid drugs to Stacey to accelerate his vital organ growth further. It was as though they suggested we could speed up development in some messing-with-nature way.

Due to his ongoing struggle inside of Stacey, his survival clock was ticking. How was this all going to work?

Another doctor explained that every hour of every day in the womb—longer via this massive series of steroid infusions—could improve his chances slightly. The organs might grow rapidly enough this way to give him and them more to work with after being removed from Stacey and immediately placed on life-saving machinery.

The entire conversation was speculative, though.

How could drugs speed up organ growth so quickly in such a short amount of time? Those steroids had to be pretty darn powerful if true. No one could even conclusively say how much growth by administering this kind of treatment might be expected in *our* case. Each is unique and has different challenges when you do something like this.

Why not just cut to the chase and deliver the baby rather than waste another twenty-four hours?

This situational remedy came at us like a sudden shock to our practical thinking, as it would for anyone. It was a long shot and borderline hard to accept as feasible, almost crazy. No other options came forth, as we quickly knew this to be the only one still on the table.

Having never heard of such a thing during pregnancy, the confident business guy I had become was automatically skeptical and super nervous about this new direction. My anxiety wasn't going to change a thing; it would only make supporting my wife more complicated.

When desperation beckons, you eventually grasp at anything. Our hopes of this working were a bit unrealistic, but it was all we had. Due to the short window presented, there was no time to reconcile any of this on our terms, either.

Doing nothing meant the baby would not survive. Understanding this, we agreed and proceeded under their direction with little to no resistance. They were headstrong on injecting my wife the following morning. Oh, joy.

The final kicker to all of this was that they would also deliver the baby one day after this steroid act.

Essentially what the entire day had now come down to was that Stacey and I were convinced to place our short-term faith in saving the life of a micro-preemie by relying upon much of the same substance people in a locker room shoot in their ass cheeks for an entirely different reason. Just fabulous.

To get this straight...we were about to inject super powerful steroid drugs into an unborn baby and his momma tomorrow (Thursday).

There was no guarantee their effects would still make any difference in the larger picture, but there was no other medical option.

The day after (Friday), they planned to have our son taken from the womb three months early and then pretend that all would somehow work out as planned.

Or, we could pray for a miracle and do nothing.

There it all was; there we were.

Everything was now out of order, twisted, and nonsensical. In two days, we went from having a routine check-up to removing a baby three months early.

Only the Morrisons.

By three o'clock, I needed to head home and pick up Aryn from his daycare. As usual, the gridlock caused an absolute disaster due to the game. It was an appropriate stressor to cap everything off that afternoon.

Taking it slow from crosswalk to crosswalk, I was processing the day somewhat while listening to music stopped at the traffic light. Glancing to my left and seeing the ballpark from the driver's seat, I tried aimlessly to accept this insane steroid information. There was so much to think about and even obsess over while I drove home.

Understand, I live in the Northeast of the country; there are no cowboys anywhere up here, and certainly not in metro Boston. Occasionally, a cop might be on a horse during an event for crowd control, but this is about as close as we come.

With sudden laser focus, I watched a little boy in black boots and plastic spurs wearing a sheriff badge walking beside his momma. She was trying to straighten out his crooked cowboy hat and neckerchief while crossing the street in front of my car. While glancing over at me, I swear he tipped his head just a bit in the form of a nod.

Go figure.

Everyone else around these two was dressed in Sox baseball attire.

Nothing made sense today.

Howdy, partner.

SECOND INNING

* * *

REVENGE

Have you ever seen a drowning person turn blue after sinking to the bottom of a swimming pool? The skin assumes something visual, with a unique color designated to represent it. "One Step Away From Death" might be an appropriate moniker.

Trust me, it ain't pretty.

A man walked to the edge and dove in to cool off; no one thought anything of it. Minutes later, there was a piercing scream from a bystander as the same overweight person now rested on the bottom, lifeless.

The sixteen-year-old, fully clothed boy, one-third of this adult's total weight, jumped in to attempt and save his life. Though a stranger to the man, it is what anyone would do.

Right place, right time, or wrong place, wrong time? It depends on how you consider it. Either way, the trauma of being involved will remain with this boy for his entire life.

The deepest part of the pool was seven feet to the bottom, exactly where the man bounced slightly from the concrete without showing signs of a struggle.

By all initial accounts, his life was over.

The skinny blond swam down to the bottom and placed his arms as best as he could around the massive midsection of this human log. With both feet on the bottom and crouching, the underage youth sprung off, hoping the upward motion of his body, coupled with the buoyancy of the water, would bring this massive sea creature to the surface.

Unfortunately, the middle-aged drowning man was still very heavy. There was no flailing or mutual aid, just a limp body being dragged to the surface and then ultimately over to the shallow end by the exhausted kid.

With one arm under each of his pits, the boy, using all his strength, lifted this guy up and over the pool edge with the aid of two other people.

On his back, the man with the blueish-purple face began to receive CPR immediately for several minutes. Up and down, his chest was compressed, and air was forced into his mouth. Over and over, this was repeated while the scared, soaking-wet boy stood there shaking in horror. The reality of what had happened settled in as he hoped his adrenaline would subside.

As if by some miracle, the dead man began to cough repeatedly after a minute and then vomited a stream of foamy alcohol and water out from the left side of his mouth. It ran down his cheek and pooled under his large head and face. There was a lot of it coming up. His lungs were full.

Color slowly returned, and the man miraculously survived.

A few sips of water later, while sitting up, he asked what had happened. Chuckling during his inquiry, he behaved like the ordeal had been nothing. Did he understand how close he was to not living?

He wasn't fazed to learn his existence here had been saved.

After adding several dismissive comments to minimize the entire occurrence further, the still light-headed fellow rose to his feet, smirked while shaking his head, and walked away.

The beer-bellied fatty was all but expired had it not been for the quick actions of a shy, blond kid who made it a point to help this man cheat **Death.**

No acknowledgment of appreciation was ever given.

In *Heavenly Pease,* I spoke about many previous personal horrible encounters right up to the end of the book, where Stacey and I were threatened with the potential passing of our unborn child.

"the all too familiar cloaked-man-of-finality, this time, was nearer to me than ever."

I lied right there in that last line.

Death was as near to me some thirty-nine years ago when I jumped in and saved that ungrateful man's life on that day, too.

It has been taunting me ever since.

Unfortunately, the actual reality is that I've been **Death's** bitch now for most of my life. There is no way to figure out why. Perhaps it started with my saving this man and allowing him to cheat a dirt nap. For some reason, I was selected long, long ago. It just worked out this way for me.

The role offers no bargaining; ownership was assigned without negotiation or conditions.

Under **Death's** control, I am just a traumatized marionette dangling by a series of emotionally charged strings called upon at a moment's notice to respond. He flaunts randomness around me as often as a laugh is needed. Certainly not by choice; my reactions are somehow amusing to him.

More pain, more fear, more risk, more anger, more faces, more ages, more sorrow, more circles, more suicide, and more creative ways.

Another loss, another puppet show dance from Aric.

And so it goes.

Never disappoint the dark one.

BIGTOP

THURSDAY, MAY 4

It's somewhat ironic how they presented to us a *possibility* delivered in the form of an ultra-powerful drug. You don't typically consider steroids as being something used to help out in a scenario such as ours. I know that's why, initially, it was hard for me to accept. Then again, what happened the day before was so quick; there wasn't any time to rationalize the details associated with what was presented. Unbelievably, my wife was already in full steroid mode when I showered earlier anyway.

This liquid crap was in her to the point of no return.

On my drive to the city, I pictured it flowing into our baby, too, knowing that it was racing through his veins, doing whatever bizarre things it does to a metabolism. If this were normal, it might be done more often and become mainstream. To the best of my knowledge, it isn't.

Beginning at nine that morning, Stacey and I spent the next three hours with a team of professionals for another urgency-filled day.

Each was ripe with new medical consults, which put our situation into perspective more deeply. Numerous dragged-out scenarios of how complex things were for our baby were presented repeatedly like an audio tape.

For the second straight morning, we discussed the potential welfare of our baby unrelentingly, always returning to the statement, "It was just so early," and their not having much promise of normalcy to share with us.

They simultaneously hurled startling information at us like thousands of ninety-mile-per-hour fastballs. Each one referred to the possibilities and probabilities we might face upon his birth tomorrow. Indirectly, they reiterated that our battle hadn't even begun if he survived.

Here, we couldn't lose sight of saving a baby's life who might otherwise have the quality of one that may or may not have been worth living in the first place. It's such an awesome way to begin your day. They were all but telling us our son might be born a circus freak.

At least, this is how *I* viewed what they were saying. I'm unsure how Stacey took this news, but it's probably similar to me.

The morning agenda ranged from the likelihood of our baby being born with risks for cerebral palsy, brain bleeding, deafness, blindness, spinal curvatures, cystic fibrosis, chronic lung disease, audio deficiencies, physical deformities, and instant heart and lung failure, to name a few.

Imagine sitting there as we had done; what do you do or say to any of this as it repeatedly smashes you in the face?

Many of these scenarios were already presented the previous day, so hearing them all a second time slightly minimized the initial shock factor, thankfully. Yet it is still rough to sit there wondering what might happen. It is hard to do because nothing is held back regarding information shared and the possibilities of what might be wrong.

We were quickly experienced in this lesson early on with Aryn, but it still isn't any easier a second time. You never harden when listening to bad news about the health of one of your flesh and blood.

It makes zero difference after accepting prematurity, dwarfism, body regulation, hydrocephalus, a ruptured placenta, Down syndrome, spina bifida, and anencephaly, as we had already done in the past. You still break down emotionally every time these realities are presented to you.

Nothing we were hearing was positive.

In each of these consultations, I noted the phrase, "In the event the baby survives the birth."

Each presenter repeatedly used these eight words as if speaking from some pre-written script. I found this suspect almost to the point that I wondered if they were trying to tell us our baby would probably not make it subtly.

Were they preparing us for misfortune in a sensitive way?

Probably so, as we segued into grief counseling for the last hour of morning consults after learning there was less than a twenty-percent chance of survival for a pregnancy like ours. Ultimately, the steroids today and scheduled early delivery tomorrow morning might still prove fruitless.

The same as earlier, we heard it all again in the afternoon and then more. Until yesterday, neither of us knew fully what we might expect to have a child miraculously surviving such a premature timetable and low birth weight. To say we were being schooled would be right.

There were so many developmental risks and subsequent intellectual delays for us to be still made aware of; without a notebook, it was hard to keep it all in check between yesterday, this morning, and now during these afternoon presentations.

Specialists took their time to further present us with additional unpleasant medical abnormalities that may have been overlooked the previous day. Being as thorough as possible during a crisis such as ours is necessary, but holy Christ, there is only so much two expecting parents can take over two days. Seriously.

We must have met with fifteen to twenty more medical professionals when all was said and done. Each seemed to pick up right where the last had left off, like a well-rehearsed stage drama. Their theming was all the same yet conveyed to us by different voices.

This grouping spoke to a new variety of concerns, ranging from blindness to deafness, limb deformities, brain damage, and heart failure. This is a really dismal set for us to think about, too, just in case the others weren't quite dramatic enough.

The most unforeseen turn was when we were coached regarding the potential need for institutional living. They made it sound as if our baby would be summarily committed to a life of dependent care, to the point of recommending a facility nearby.

Stacey and I toured it weeks later. (More on this in another chapter and book.)

All you can do is listen while knowing you remain entirely at the mercy of conversation and statistical odds. For me, it was like picking up the phone repeatedly to be made aware that my father had collapsed or receiving those calls when my employee had been murdered. Today, there is no difference between any of them.

Thankfully, this onslaught of words concluded late that Thursday afternoon after six merciless hours. After hearing about all the potential circumstances representative of delivering a premature child our size, we couldn't have taken more anyway.

Overall, it had been lousy. A who's who of biting informational sources visited us one after the other. Dutifully, they delivered an Academy Award-winning presentation of surreal information.

Kudos to them all. What a performance. Professionally, they did what they were expertly trained to do.

The rest of this was on our baby.

Anxiety ruled the stage before today; it did so now again for these endless hours. For me, it was inescapable. The build-up was mounting even more, knowing that upon my son's birth tomorrow, many of these horrific scenarios would answer themselves and play out fully right there in the delivery room.

It wasn't until the last consult that I asked the primary doctor during his recap this most straightforward question from deep within my heart:

> "You and your teams have spent two days telling us bad things. Do you have some good words to say that might offer us positive encouragement here? Can you share anything to give us some hope through this? Anything at all?"

Making it a point, he looked each of us straight in the eyes while moving his head back and forth, back and forth, almost like a Disney animatronic. His actions alone let me know what was coming.

Replying in only one word, he responded, "No."

DRAIN

I n the end, we settled quietly back into Stacey's hospital room, trying to process all we had heard. A routine, unfortunately, by then between the two boys, all too familiar. At some point, it may have been nice never to need to do this again.

The only noise came from a lightbulb buzzing slightly over her bed and from someone tapping on a keyboard at the station outside our door.

The stillness inside our room was at odds with the hustle and bustle below us on the street.

Each could hear the other person breathing; no words were coming from our mouths yet.

There was nothing to say.

Neither of us possessed the courage to speak for several minutes for what I believe was in fear of saying the wrong thing or coming across as resigned to what everyone there seemed to think was impending.

Two people sat alone in another hospital room.

I was trying to understand why life kept insisting on kicking my shins. At the same time, Stacey was probably scared out of her mind to unfold the potential complexities of tomorrow.

There was to be no escaping the morning. No hiding in music, memories, or casual talk with a buddy to soften this reality. Our child would be born in less than twenty-four hours, ready or not.

In reality, we had gone from beating insurmountable probabilities earlier in the winter to hearing that our past victories might still have been for nothing in the long run.

Whatever was coming, we had to accept it for what it was. The actual outcome was entirely out of our hands now.

For the umpteenth time, the Morrison family course was newly uncharted. We had done our best. For sure, tomorrow was going to be one hell of a day.

Getting up from the bed and walking over to the window, the setting sun outside captured my focus. I stared off into cloudiness for a dozen or so empty seconds.

Looking out at absolutely nothing and everything simultaneously, I mouthed the words "God Dammit" quietly and desperately under my breath.

It was just loud enough that Stacey heard it, too.

FUR

The fun part of living life at my age is carefully rifling through years of baggage and being capable of accepting all the positives for what they were: wonderfully innocent experiences to enjoy forever. It is evident by now how much importance I place on my past and its lessons for me today.

In addition to the memories of happier days, I want to mention the impact that certain people can have during our earlier years, too.

Each of us has a few longstanding friends who have influenced our backstories. Some travel alongside our birthdays for decades, while others find space with new folks and fade out like dusk sunshine.

Hopefully, none ever leave you entirely by physical presence; if so, there is resolution in that they cannot remove themselves from those past years spent with us. These participants help guide many of our reflections as well. It is vital to remain in contact, even by making a simple phone call.

One of mine is a pal from a long time ago named Jeff. He is a close friend that I have known since the third grade and, in many ways, has become a part of our family; ask him, and he will tell you!

To say he is a "character" is not doing Jeffrey justice.

Invariably, the holidays bring him back as if he has never left. Somehow, he appears at Thanksgiving or Christmas each year to enjoy a free meal without an invite and remind us of his familiar status. This guy can eat pie, holy cow. And please don't even get me started about his choice of gifts!

Someone once referred to Jeff as having a unique ability to talk a dog off a bone truck. He is always there when I need to smile a little, so this quality isn't necessarily a bad thing *some* of the time. However, because of the inherent length of our chats, I regularly need to be fully aware of my schedule before calling.

Most conversations between us will undoubtedly be humorous. Jeff is an incredible resource for this, as we tend to act like two teenagers all over again when in each other's company.

We were even referred to by our boss as "two juvenile delinquents" once. He scolded our asses while Jeff and I did anything and everything to not look at each other for fear of bursting out in laughter.

When we speak on the phone or in person, a few probable discussion areas always become a part of the conversation. Sometimes, I am barely in the mood to go there, but somehow, he inserts them into the inanest sentences. He has made it a verbal art form.

Among these are his apparent need to volunteer unwanted details on his irritable bowel situation and update me on the large amounts of hair he has growing all over his body. Lest I also forget, he finds it necessary to bring up stories that never seem to be in my recollection bank.

Most of the time, I listen for a few minutes and quickly try to change the subject!

It is hard to believe that two relatively stable folks can still become so immature almost instantly within each other's company. But like magic, the transformation seems to happen as soon as we speak. To this day, when we get together and recount some of our mischievous encounters from days gone by, we typically laugh so hard that it hurts every time.

Another one of his many mysteries is routinely leaving me many text messages at three in the morning. What Jeff does at that time of day is unknown to everyone. I subscribe to the "don't ask, don't tell" philosophy.

With him, this information is better left unsaid.

As I mentioned, many experiences from my past can make me smile. Unquestionably, this guy has been with me for many of the funniest occasions a person might ever experience in this life.

After elementary school, we used to venture out and set his model airplanes on fire in the leaves and sticks next to a stone wall surrounding our playground. We'd sit together and watch the melting plastic drip while continuously disfiguring what was once a well-crafted toy, thinking this was the most incredible visual ever.

We enjoyed seeing them cook without ever considering what we were doing in terms of risk. The burning occurred on a dry forest bed with leaves and twigs all around, ready to catch fire, too! We were one hearty gust of wind away from this becoming a reality. We might have set the entire woods ablaze!

Perched upon two rocks without care, we unthinkingly risked firetrucks and mayhem, all in the name of experimentation.

Two juvenile delinquents, alright.

Over time, we made a calculated upgrade from burning model planes in the fifth grade to soaking tennis balls, lighting them, and playing catch. I have no idea how this brilliant idea came about, but we were instantly hooked on a newer version of Fun with Fire. A new game that we affectionally named "Fireball."

Do not try this at home.

The goal was to saturate a tennis ball with lighter fluid from a plastic squirt bottle and then light it up. Amazingly, as the liquid covering it burns, you can touch the ball without getting hurt.

Acting like two brainless idiots, we tossed it back and forth as the fluid began to burn off. Over time, catching the ball becomes a lot more difficult because your hand starts to respond to the flame of fire as the once fuzzy skin around it begins to sizzle up on its own without the aid of this accelerant.

Each time the ball was caught from that point, our hands began to burn. You quickly needed to grab it and return it to the other knucklehead playing the game or your palm was at risk of getting cooked. The first person to tap out from the pain was declared the loser.

Indeed, it is a brilliant thing to do in your spare time.

What a couple of silly geniuses we were!

We always ended up heading home with burns across our hands from playing this ridiculous game while laughing wildly at each other.

I am sharing this with you to highlight a simple truth.

As important as reaching back and enjoying our past shadows, it is equally important to never lose sight of the people who assisted in creating them.

I know this now.

THIRD INNING

* * *

HOMEWORK

While reviewing many of the most important details about our uncertain prognosis in front of the fireplace, I could tell what Mom was thinking by the look on her face. The emphasis I directed here was more on the mortality of our child and less on what physically might be wrong with him.

She was preparing for the worst and hardly listening to much else of what I had to share anyway. As I look back now, that's probably not a bad thing.

It worked out nicely that my mother was at our house because it was comforting to have emotional support sitting in that living room with me. She had already placed Aryn to bed and awaited an update upon my arrival. I believe she is the only person on my side of the family who knew what we were dealing with. Being the guarded person I am, until now, I never shared this stuff with anyone else.

With her as the exception, I told no one.

By sparing Mom most of the conversations we'd constantly heard over the last forty-eight hours, I attempted to make small talk before opening my laptop. Due to this delivery being so early, our baby didn't even have a name yet.

Out of necessity, I needed to embark upon the most appropriate search imaginable to decide what this baby would be called. His birth was in the morning, so no time was wasted.

The discovery of his perfect name would proudly reflect my most outstanding work. This job had to be achieved with total perfection as it would become the legacy of a unique child.

Until now, we hadn't even considered one. His original birthdate was still three months away!

Since Stacey was not home with me to do this research, we wouldn't benefit from discussing any potential matches. This task, which we agreed on before leaving the hospital earlier, was all on me. Everything was in a rush anyway; as long as one of us was on this project, it was all good.

The process began with me searching hundreds of names on the Internet, hoping to find one that might represent his true spirit as we had sensed it. It wouldn't be easy to match him with exactly the most fitting one, but I knew eventually, it would all fit into place.

While talking casually to my mom, I continuously searched my laptop, reviewing name after name but not finding anything close to what I had hoped for. It took an entire hour to sort through several dozen and then dismiss them because none felt right. I hoped it would connect instantly when the right one came to me.

There were still plenty of hours left until morning to find it, if need be. Heck, I wouldn't be able to sleep at all anyway.

Mom and I reviewed so many more, but it became almost exhausting in some ways. But when you remind yourself of the importance of what you are doing, the depleted energy quickly fills back up again. I knew it would come. Time was still on our side.

"Kayden" was the last one in the final string of names I researched almost accidentally. I originally wanted "Aiden," but the words defaulted to this one.

After the other groupings bombed, I was not optimistic that this one would provide many worthy opportunities. Still, I entered more details in the search box to learn more about it.

As the page loaded, I first noticed that this name had come back reflecting not one but two origins, which instantly made it some-what unique for that reason alone.

It described the name as having Arabic and American roots, each possessing different meanings.

The first origin of Arabic was *companion, friend.*

I liked this one already!

The name seemed appropriate because I had felt that based on the journey this baby had already taken us on, one of his same messages was comfort.

Had our son been trying to tell us that he was somehow a companion for us, providing support? It sounds nice, but I am sure it was my own wishful thinking.

The description stated: "He reserves his heart for friends and family. Determined, Kayden can weather any storm."

This one was perfect; so far, so good.

The American meanings of the name were *strong-willed* and *fighter*.

Interpreting this one was easy, too.

Our baby had already shown that he represented those words several times; there was no confusion here. This kid was persistent.

Again, this meaning captured our son's essence, too.

Goosebumps were felt as I reread the characteristics associated with this one several times before concluding that my search was suddenly over; there was no doubt.

This name symbolized everything we wanted from it!

The internet could have provided hundreds more words for me to consider that evening, but I knew none would come close to this perfect match between philosophy and reality.

When you know it, you know it. I had found absolutely the most appropriate name to call our son!

Finally, in my family, the unique nature of spelling a name is an expressive way to highlight one's individuality to the world. Aryn and I both have very nontraditional spellings for ours; this child also needed to have a twist to his.

Naming our kids was a part of the dream early on in my big-picture marriage vision, so it became as essential to determine the spelling as the name itself.

After removing the Y, there it was.

I accomplished some of my most meaningful work at 10:43 on Thursday night, May 4, 2006.

Mom agreed as I poured another glass of wine for myself to celebrate and attempt to quell my nerves. In a few hours, our son was going to be cut from the womb. Who the hell knew what we were in for?

He was officially named Kaden Harding Morrison tonight.

Unfortunately, I also knew that this name might be significant in becoming representative of heaven's newest angel.

K-A-D-E-N

DISCLOSURE

I've always had a few weird hang-ups. People don't know of them because this complicated guy keeps them close to the vest. There are so many that I refuse you to bore by detailing them.

Briefly, here is one of mine:

I do have an aversion to a certain number. Thankfully, it never became a part of this story. For fifty-five years, I have not allowed it in any way to force me into breaking my beliefs. It influences my actions today unhealthily in the form of avoidance behaviors. I can't use that numbered gas pump, the check-out stations, begin or end any task when the clock displays this digit, and I certainly will never make any crucial decisions on this day of the month either.

What a mess I am!

Think about how time-consuming and highly frustrating living a life of constant avoidance might be. Many others can relate to how obsessively tricky it is to have movement throughout a typical day dictated by performing certain rituals under the umbrella of having OCD. The entire premise is to not break specific patterns for the fear of doing so suddenly creating lousy luck. You know exactly how this works if you have daily routines governing your actions. My number thing used to drive my wife crazy.

How does this all fit in with the story?

Remember when I found two pennies on that dry pavement spot in February? Once I placed them both into my back pocket that day, they instantly became another part of my obsessive behavior. In my head, soon after finding them, probably the next morning, it made sense for them to play a role somehow in all of this. Was it just a form of random luck they were found?

Somehow, I became convinced my doing so was all a part of the grand plan. I believed it back then and still do today.

Upon waking and getting dressed each morning, I collected those two coins off the nightstand where I had placed them the evening before and carefully put them into my back-right pocket for luck. They remained with me daily without gaps, as some form of hidden inspiration and good fortune. By doing this faithfully, my mind convinced me that with each new sunrise, if I carried them, all would turn out alright for the day.

As the previous one had its influence, another day with those two coins was about gaining positive momentum so our son could be born without complications.

There is a particular building of energy when you stack up days in succession without anything suddenly causing you to fall. Based on the last three days Stacey and I had spent hearing all that terrible crap, the pennies were even more valuable as I sat there seeking comfort from them.

Psychologically, dressing with them each day made sense if I could somehow attribute our future progress to lucky coin influence. I often heard them clinking together when I walked or proceeded upstairs or got out of my car. The sound was faint, but it was a welcome validation. I often reached back to touch them for additional luck when my mind drifted to a darker place.

The ultimate bigger-picture goal of the pennies was to carry them with me until the day our son was born. There was no plan for them after. I guess they symbolized **Hope** to me for a finite amount of time. In short, they were my crutch to capture it and somehow attempt to manipulate it in our favor.

Maybe my head was clouded, and I had been open to challenging things unconventionally, but who cared?

I thought, *Why not continue placing them in my back pocket daily? Where was the harm if it made me feel better?*

We had already come far when I found them on the pavement outside the restaurant beneath my car door.

Who cares if our chances to believe in nearly impossible things had come down to the power of luck in those two clinking, heads-up pennies?

No one knew they existed but me, anyway.

I guess it might have been a button, a picture on a piece of paper, or even a lucky bullet. (I will leave that one for another day.) Two pennies gave me something to believe in—the potential for my son to be born alive and that all would turn out well.

Yes, I realize this chapter reads like the words of a madman. Formulate your opinions as you feel appropriate.

After reading an article on how some people have certain acts they perform in various circumstances to avoid bad luck (in their minds), the magic bell of enlightenment almost instantly rang in my head. Indeed, I was like many of those people! When your back is against the wall, as ours were, you grasp for whatever seems appropriate to help get one leg up on uncertainty.

But then again, we make wishes before blowing candles, hang horseshoes, select the number seven, do not allow the groom to see his bride early on the wedding day, and consider it magic to see falling stars.

We place holy water on a forehead, bring trinkets to bingo, collect clovers, avoid breaking mirrors, use predictable phrases, clutch rabbits' feet, kiss the Blarney Stone, and wear specific clothing pieces to sporting events, all in the name of luck.

In baseball, the practice of turning a ball cap inside out and then placing it back upon your head is somehow believed to alter the course of the game. Now and then, you may watch the camera pan slowly on a dugout full of players with their hats gently sitting on top of their heads in this way—an entire bench of visual silliness on display.

On second thought, perhaps carrying two pennies isn't so ridiculous after all.

WET

FRIDAY, MAY 5, 2006

T oday was the day. It wasn't going to be like any other. Shortly after, we were about to find out what God, if there was such a being, had ultimately planned for us with this child.

It was a complicated one emotionally on so many different levels. We hoped to get through it and come out on the other side with some degree of peace, but at what cost? The stakes were high, and the odds were low.

There are aspects of life that make no logical sense, and they never will. I have concluded that we must accept this as accurate rather than attempt to dissect why our years are filled with so many inconsistencies.

What about them causes humankind to twist in discomfort upon every sudden divergent pass?

When trouble appears on the horizon, we instantly become

uneasy. Though we face so many unknowns throughout our time on this planet, why this happens still seems strange.

I have learned to accept that lessons are born through our experiences rather than questioning their purpose or shaking with trepidation when they loom. Doing this can work wonders during adversity.

This is all well and good when you have time to look back and consider what you have been through. As rough days happen in real time, an entirely different set of rules plays out. Nervousness and panic become the newest pals to join the party. For me, they were inside and ever-present on May 5, 2006.

On this off-kilter Friday, it was a colder-than-usual day for the month, appearing scripted so that the sun was nowhere to be seen. If it were possible to remain asleep for a year and stop time from marching, I'd have been the first to make it happen rather than face the fast-approaching fateful hours.

Appropriately, the lack of color in the sky made for a perfect, desolate backdrop. On this storyboard, nothing else would suffice. Almost as if by foreboding design, the drabness around Boston seemed to complement the melancholy emotional feel the rain had brought overhead.

I'm not sure it would have made sense to pretend I was somehow optimistic based on how things suddenly unfolded over the last three days. We were facing some hard driving pressure without question. This morning represented the crescendo of our what-if scenarios.

Living with anxiety for so long has taught me its powerful grip and the tricks it can play on an already overly obsessive brain. I was stronger now and refused to go back there willingly, but a mental slide down today would prove inevitable. This unfortunate set of complications was a lot for anyone to deal with.

I reviewed all the bad things that might happen in that delivery room, so much so that my mind was filled with terrible flashes during the entire drive to Boston. A new consideration did arise for every mile I drove closer to Boston.

Having so many dark thoughts simultaneously is unnatural and severely jarring. They just kept appearing over and over again in force over everything else that might have come their way. They were inescapable.

No matter how often I played my favorite songs to fit the mood, I couldn't stop them. Floating from the present for three minutes and twenty seconds per song might have been excellent.

This one-time vital emotional crutch of mine blending lyrics and notes had now fled the scene, leaving me only with the vapors of mortality to fill up the space in my car.

Ruinous pondering was all I had at the moment.

There needed to be some clarity for a few items still left undone in the bigger picture of the morning, so I made a simple list in my head of questions to ask when I got there:

• *If Kaden did not survive his birth, what are the rules of conduct regarding seeing, touching, or even holding him?*

• *Would they attempt to whisk him away like he was some tragic afterthought or just another of life's unfair misfortunate endings?*

• *Would they align properly with us, knowing we would need much time to grieve in his presence should the unthinkable happen?*

I sure as hell knew if Kaden was going to be stillborn or even come out alive and then pass away suddenly, there needed to be an opportunity to hold him.

• *Would they attempt to take him away immediately for fear of traumatization?*

It would never be suitable for us to be denied a handful of fleeting moments with him. Alive or not, he was still our baby Kaden, son and Aryn's brother.

If you were holding your lifeless baby in your arms, would you ever want to let it go, knowing you would never touch it again?

I wanted to be able to cradle him tightly for Aryn's sake. To allow his body to feel all the love we shared for him. Even if only for the briefest of time.

This might be the only memory with him afforded to us—one which just couldn't be missed due to procedure or oversight in the delivery room. He deserved to acquire our love in the rawest of forms.

And, if our baby was ultimately going to leave us, at the very least, I wanted to be aware of the moment his gentle spirit was lifted from this world.

• *How was this going to be communicated?*

I was having some seriously dark contemplations here, but they were all so freaking real and relevant based on where we were headed. You are never prepared to ask or seek the answers to these questions. But obviously, I felt that I had to.

Nothing about the delivery would be typical or routine; this information was owed based on our circumstances, just in case. I was focused on preventing him from becoming another check mark or casualty to some uncaringly rigid protocol.

Was any of this too much to ask?

The Nimbostratus cloud blanket couldn't have been any more perfect by the time I arrived. One that was casting a murky, dank gloom down upon Boston Children's and the entire city. It was a movie set, and we were the players getting ready for the big scene.

While walking toward the buildings, the magnitude of our situation continued to build even more within me. As if the long car ride down hadn't been enough, the awareness of being here now was kicking the ass of this ever-loving family man.

For the less than fortunate who can relate, a day like today is a pure, unadulterated trip to brain bleakness. Once again, I was caught in a stranglehold.

Before, there had been hours to put off this unthinkable sequence that was about to happen. Suddenly, here it was, with no turning back. I was at the hospital, and the anxious shit was partying inside of me. Pouring a cocktail of answered questions for all in attendance.

Approaching the glass entrance cautiously, I paced back and forth in the common area outside the hospital before heading up to visit my wife.

A perfect strategy became clear as I marched in a circle for a second to work it out in my head quickly.

Later, depending on what was in store for us, I could always duck back outside and mix any sorrowful tears with these raindrops without appearing so miserably obvious in my grief. Doing so might potentially make a convenient excuse for having those watery eyes. Stacey might never know.

Filing this knowledge away, I put the game face on as the elevator brought me to her floor.

This was my plan.

Blame it on the rain.

SHARE

I came off stage about a week ago and was greeted by a woman who asked me to share how I handle difficult conversations. This question doesn't require much thought for me to formulate a response. Because there have been so many of them through the years, I now have a wealth of tips learned. While everyone is unique due to the nature of the content, it takes some time to become better versed.

My response was, "It depends on the situation itself." Adversity is a busy word. It can be as ambiguous as anything and quite specific at the same time. When your entire life is built around it, one tends to apply various forms of the word on a scale.

This chapter outlines one of the more unique adversity twists in this story. It was quick, but because it came out of nowhere suddenly, it racked up some credibility based on its impact. Stacey and I were suddenly asked to have a life-or-death conversation in her hospital room about ten minutes after my arrival.

It was weighty and forced upon us without any chance for prep or notice. There was enough pressure in and of itself to mentally prepare for the unknown that surrounded the birth less than an hour away. Then they sprung another last-minute gem on us.

There should be more time to come to such a necessary conclusion rather than having it thrust upon you at a weaker point. Had they told us about this yesterday, we might have used the evening to gather our respective points of view to share in the morning. Now, there wasn't much time to do this exercise justice.

Most people never have to imagine themselves sitting alongside their spouses while conversing about their survival and the potential of never seeing them alive again within the next sixty minutes.

We had to.

Until now, we never considered her condition problematic to any degree of concern. Precisely, they needed me to give the order to save her life at the expense of potentially losing the baby or tell them to save him and then risk losing my wife.

Think about that one for a moment.

It was blindsiding while trying to have a few calm moments before the procedure was forced into having such a unique deliberation between us. Naturally, all possible efforts are always made to preserve both lives under duress, but some decisions must be made in advance due to protocol.

Since Stacey was about to have another c-section, we had falsely assumed that things with her would be similarly uneventful in the process, like our first delivery. We never had this consideration when Aryn was delivered, so it wasn't even on our radar until now.

Sure, she had been deteriorating gradually, but not to the degree of necessitating any life-saving decision-making orders.

From here, depending upon either condition becoming dire in the delivery room, whatever direction we decided in advance would immediately become the standing order later should it come to it. The choice was to have them save her or the baby. Ultimately, it was up to me to articulate our wishes.

There was undoubtedly an unpleasantness to it all. A shift from the risk of losing the baby within the next hour had now become two potential losses, at the very most, for consideration.

In that swirl of uncertainty, we also had to account for this decision's impact on Aryn. If they could only save the baby, he would forever hold me responsible for taking his momma away.

In such a decision-making role, you must be prepared to live with the choices made. There is no turning back, no option to pass, no advanced warning, no time to deliberate, no sleeping on it, no guarantees, no coaching, no references, and most importantly, no changes for any reason once the order is given.

Just before heading in for the birth of our second son, we were now conversing about her fate, that of his, and of my being a widowed, single dad and the father to only one.

Even as I type this today, I never felt Stacey was at risk. When a doctor forces you to have this discussion, serious stuff automatically changes your rational thinking.

Was it possible I could lose my wife within the next hour, also?

The entire forced conversation between us was still very out of body. There was no television, radio, or everyday background distractions present. She shared her thoughts, and I did the same with mine. Our time together here was one of the most upended ever. We were talking about **Death** becoming as natural as the air to one or both of them.

Only two people on the planet can share this part of the morning in detail if asked: Stacey and myself. The eye contact we shared during these moments is still blazed in my mind. Another reason is that sleep is my enemy.

My wife was wheeled off in her bed on the way for an epidural; I sat there staring as she moved farther from me, out the door, down the hall, and into the elevator. Stacey and our unborn, steroid-filled fighter were off preparing for their next battle.

Ultimately, the doctor bestowed the power of finality upon me.

Save Kaden, lose Stacey.

Save Stacey and lose my son.

Lose them both.

Save them both.

Only one person knows how the next chapters might have been rewritten had any part of this become a reality. His name is "Aric with an A." I live with this knowledge and wrestle it unwillingly more often than not.

Like so many others haunting me, revisiting this occurrence requires some heavy lifting. The whispers pertaining to my decision will remain locked away for now. They must stay there until I am ready to unpack and accept them.

Reasoning repeatedly before proceeding down to the assigned waiting area, I came to terms with the justification of what I would say should the unthinkable happen, hoping all the while it would ultimately become a useless exercise in morbidity.

Still, the only consolation prize for failure here was **Death.**

FOURTH INNING

* * *

THREE

Money accumulation was extremely important to me back in the day. When you don't come from it, you strive to obtain access to what it is all about. Working hard, developing a good work ethic, and investing in getting oneself to the next level are motivations for many people.

Starting with very little, it certainly was for me.

If you come from money, you never really know of losing sleep due to not having enough to get by each week or month. It is much more tiring to work your ass off accumulating wealth than waking up daily with an inherited bank account to quell your financial blues.

There are days I wish the fortunes of some people could be reversed briefly. More than a few eyes would open up to the reality of appreciating the hard-working efforts of others.

What an interesting existence between the two different perspectives, but when facing the mortality of an unborn child, neither holds any weight. Money means nothing, riches are useless, and social status has zero value. The fact that you come from nothing doesn't make you any more deserving of a break here, either.

This morning, I would have gladly welcomed homelessness and pennilessness if it guaranteed a positive outcome within the next two hours. As I have communicated repeatedly throughout these two books, however, you can't influence **Fate;** it owns each of us.

Two doors swung into a waiting area just outside the delivery room. I recall looking straight ahead out the nearest window before sitting down. The raindrops jogged down the pane in front of me almost incessantly, like in a marathon. They were present in a manner reminiscent of random tears running steadily down a madman's face. I stared at them for a second or seventy; the imagery was curious. My short-term goal was to look at anything, keep my mind busy, and avoid the obvious.

This was precisely what I needed.

Plastic chairs were up against the wall to my right. The nurse led me to this area to remain while they continued the epidural and prepped Stacey. Just minutes before, a final look from her affirmed the uncertainty that lay ahead beyond the doors a few feet away. They in no way represented a welcome sight to me.

I thoughtfully selected the middle chair in this row of only three. Melting down upon it was a man who could have used guidance from his dad. Instead of being alone in my thoughts, scared for my family, and woefully helpless to influence the outcome, his presence might have eased my condition.

For the next few minutes, I sat with both of my feet on the floor, my head hanging low, and my eyes not focused on anything but the pattern of the tiles below.

Then, at the top right corner, another raindrop ran down and across the pane to the bottom. It could have been any drop on any window, but it temporarily allowed me to focus on something other than the floor.

The random course it assumed while streaking its way down slowly seemed to connect with me briefly in some arbitrary way. It was determined and purposeful. Precisely as I should have felt before heading into the delivery room, I wasn't even close.

I was just the opposite. Afraid and scared of what was about to occur.

There was a bustle of medical professionals around me, to which I paid no attention. At the moment, I was entirely focused on the immediate concerns for my wife and child, nothing else.

Words read from a piece on how important it is to maintain a constant oxygen flow while facing stressful situations seemed, in theory, to apply well. It all sounded good, but no one cares about being deliberate or steady when facing terror. It is all about the moment. Screw the article.

My breathing was pronounced while I muscle-jellied in my seat, no more dignified than a dog panting in the summer sun.

My body was as unfamiliar as I could ever recall it. No trip to a massage parlor would have fixed the bundle of knots called a spine, either.

My entire sense of being was in disarray as I glanced up toward the window for a third time and watched the path of another rain-drop break apart down the pane.

A distinct tingly feeling returned. My hundred million needles were present from my head, down my body, to my feet. I didn't care about any of these physical manifestations for the first time ever. None of this day was about me. It was all about Stacey and Kaden.

There I sat in the middle of three chairs with what seemed to be an encore of final thoughts racing through my mind, but without having any singular one to focus on.

How odd it seemed that I was not provided with the comfort of Stacey sitting next to me in one of those chairs or Aryn in the other.

There I sat by myself in the middle of three chairs:

• Reflecting, with growing concern, upon what Stacey must have been feeling at the moment, some fifteen feet away, with an equal number of thoughts in her mind.

• Knowing that the desperation would become even more real once I summoned the courage to enter through those two doors and into the delivery room.

• Considering over and over how Kaden had already proven the medical professionals wrong once before. It was slightly comforting to hang on to the knowledge that our child had shown tremendous resilience.

• Strategizing how my conversations with Aryn would go later that evening.

After about fifteen minutes of constant mental harassment, one of the swinging doors to my right opened as a nurse requested my presence.

Tumult would occupy me at a never-felt level once I had summoned enough courage to proceed through those doors.

I reached back to touch the two special pennies hidden in the back-right pocket of my scrubs one final time, hoping for any remaining positive energy they could muster.

In the delivery room, **Uncertainty** was panting pre-orgasmically in one corner. **Optimism** gestured reassuringly at me from the other while **Death's** shadow was cast across a portion of the room.

Ignoring them all, I sat down beside my wife.

GASP

The rest of the world continued, as usual, all around us. Business transactions, staff meetings, loading zone deliveries, and spilled drinks on shirts. Traffic, the stock market, and everything listed under the typical day classification also occurred.

Unfortunately, our day was like no other in any way.

Life and its opposite were indecisive that morning—a tug of war had ensued to claim Kaden as one of their own. This one was so unique that there was no time for our minds to go to fun and happy places. We hadn't given random care about anything but our baby. My job was irrelevant; the news, sports scores, and financial responsibilities were all cast aside. Today was all about facing something beyond description.

There were no thoughts about cute baby clothes, funny mannerisms, or tendencies to laugh at random things as most parents might do in a typical pregnancy/pre-delivery situation. It had all come down to this rather precarious moment in time. We were either going to rejoice at our blessed new gift or begin a very long healing process that may or may not prove to be something we could ever wholly deal with properly.

Stacey was on the bed, already feeling affected by whatever they gave her to relax appropriately. A female doctor entered the room, shook my hand, and remarked, "Let's have a baby."

The positive way she said the comment was reassuring in some ways, but the weight of what we were up against very quickly negated any upside reactions. She knew the severity of what we had been facing and was trying professionally to put us both at ease with this simple remark. By design, it was casual, but it sure was nice to hear nonetheless.

Was it possible Stacey and I had overreacted to everything?

Nahhhh.

The delivery process began quickly and methodically, just like when Aryn was born. The cesarean procedure was estimated to take about an hour and a half from start to completion, barring any unforeseen complications.

Once again, I was at the head of the bed near Stacey's face, very similar to where I had been for the delivery some five years prior. Instantly, we began sharing our nerves as they collectively traded bodies back and forth.

This time was different, as I visibly shook, trying not to let Stacey see my hands. I had no planned words, no reminders of days past in Meredith, and nothing imagined in advance to remove us from where we were. I obsessed with remaining in tune with every noise, word, and potential for action.

This one had an odd feel, and I was still unprepared either way.

Regretfully, if the time came, the decision Stacey and I spoke about earlier had to be given upon demand instantly. Should there be a sudden turn one way or the other, I knew I needed to become a judge, jury, and executioner. There is a lot of weight there. Aside from seeing my dad in a coma, I can't think of facing anything else heavier.

It was awful.

We remained on eggshells, but nothing noteworthy came hurling our way as we had initially feared. For the first forty-five minutes, there weren't any crisis outbursts, raised voices of concern, or anything else. While I could hear chatter and activity, it all seemed very structured and typical.

What a relief!

They underestimated what we were dealing with in terms of baby growth. The doctor spoke to us through the curtain to make us aware that our baby was even lighter than they had initially estimated at weighing three pounds. As it looked, he was even smaller.

Aryn was born prematurely at five pounds, and even then, he struggled, so we were already speculating what three pounds would bring us. Now, to find out he was less than that?

Well, that's just awesome, I thought while my heart sank deeper into my chest for a second or two.

Why worry about it?

There was nothing to be done now but continue.

"Owwww, owww, owww—I can feel that!" Stacey screamed out loud.

Her voice was pained. Since she always had a high pain threshold, whatever happened must have hurt like anything. Stacey can take a lot. Hearing her yell out startled me and, in a way, brought me back to focus.

Two forces wrestled relentlessly back and forth that morning. **UNCERTAINTY** and **OPTIMISM** continued tugging at Kaden's pure spirit this entire time.

Which one had the upper hand? I hadn't a clue.

"Someone will have a birthday very soon," the doctor said.

Was this good, bad, or the end?

While sitting on the edge of my seat for the last time, I slowly felt my heartbeat returning to a predictable cadence upon hearing this. Everything was about to be over, mercifully.

She hadn't made it feel like things were not going well, so briefly, I allowed positive imagery to play upstairs.

A mile away from Fenway Park, somewhere deep within the same brick structure that performed daily miracles, we were ready to be new parents and greet the newest Morrison in minutes.

Yes!

Might we be blessed to have made it through this without complications?

Were we about to go forth again, proving that our independent fortitude and positive energies could rebalance our familiar scales of adversity?

The answers to these questions remained a mystery. It wasn't yet time to find out.

Sixty seconds later, there was complete chaos.

WINE

In truth, my friend Jeffrey traveled along some bumpier parts of the road later in life with me, as a true friend would. He has always been there as a loyal, supportive, and trusted confidant. Because this series comprises my life experiences, not including a few funny anecdotal snippets wouldn't do this reflection justice, either.

It remains to be discovered if he was ever aware of the bad things I was exposed to as a youth back home; someday, when comfortable, it may need to be brought up. He knew about all the times at ten or eleven years of age when The Soda Shoppe in town became a temporary escape for me to sit with a plate of french fries and get away. The reasons may still be unclear to him.

Though many of my childhood friends are very near and dear to me in spirit now, Jeffrey is one I regularly still contact. He was in my wedding party when Stacey and I got married, which means a lot to me.

I mention him several times here because he, too, plays a role in my story. For this, I appreciate him beyond my ever saying it in person. I can honestly mention he was there every step of the way in some fashion during each of these books.

We had been playing with fire since third grade, as I noted. By the eighth grade, while others our age may have begun experimenting with chemical sedation, we were still fervently trying to burn each other by tossing a flaming, hot ball back and forth instead.

Brilliant.

This game mercifully ended for good one Sunday afternoon in autumn behind the same local elementary school in my neighborhood where it had all begun with the models.

After suffering the blistering effects of fire burning upon our bare skin, we decided it might be more fun to upgrade the thrills by using the brick side of the gymnasium wall to play our version of handball with one of these burning hot tennis things.

While on fire, we hit the ball against the bricks and then over to the other person. It was pretty neat to see as the flame created a smoking black fire-tail each time it gathered speed. The sight of fire bouncing back and forth off the side of a wall at night was something to behold. It was just a fantastic display.

Jeff and I were onto something here!

One night, after playing for a few minutes and thinking it was the coolest thrill ever, Jeffrey hit it so hard that it missed the edge of the brick by a mile. We watched it go up about fifteen feet into the air and then bounce once off the ground before finally landing inside the open top of a dumpster off to our left. (You can see where this is headed.)

You had better believe that the entire lot within the receptacle suddenly caught fire as the ball landed inside and rolled around, instantly lighting every flammable item that came close to it. This one was heaped full of paper, cardboard, and leaves.

In no time, it had summarily touched enough material to create a small, self-contained inferno. Flames and smoke began stretching into the air, increasing in intensity by the second.

Before long, we had made a full-on flaming spectacle, quickly at risk of becoming one hot crisis if left alone.

We had set the whole dumpster on fire in a BIG way!

Since it was a steel enclosure, it would have burned itself out anyway, but the flames, ash, and smoke, while reaching for the heavens, could have tipped off a call from a neighbor to dispatch the fire department. We couldn't take that chance.

Jeff and I immediately found ourselves diving in, trying to put out the fire with our sneakers in this confined space. It probably wasn't our brightest moment to leap into a fully ablaze container, but there was no other choice, so we did it.

Two future leaders of tomorrow began jumping around inside a dumpster that was now massively on fire due to the irresponsible actions of complete nitwits.

We may have been two jackasses stomping grapes in a huge vat; it looked like the same type of scene!

Leaping up and down as gangly kangaroos, we pounded our feet like two double-bass, drum-playing rockstars. For several tense minutes, we clumped and tapped like the fools we were to have done such an irresponsible thing in the first place.

We did everything to put the damn thing out as quickly as we could while reeling in pain as the fire char burned our soles and socks in real time beneath our knees, melting the rubber instantly off our footwear and searing it to our toes.

Hot, burning rubber hurts like hell on your skin!

There was some dripping plastic on the sliding side door to the right of the dumpster, but thankfully, after about eight minutes of very tense chaos, we took care of the bulk of the problem.

In the end, both of us were covered head to toe in black soot, our sneakers destroyed, our clothes black and torn, and our faces charred as we climbed back out, instantly rejoicing in our teenage stupidity.

If given a chance to go back and do it over, I would never elect to change a thing.

This experience was one for the books.

Each of us has a Jeffrey *influencer*, whether we elect to admit it or not. I also acknowledge that I know many other folks who claim to have an Aric *influencer* in theirs. All of whom could also tell crazy stories from the past regarding time spent in my presence.

Of course, as a parent and someone who now assumes the responsibilities of overseeing a successful business entity, I am not the same person today. Still, I sincerely accept that we should relive those carefree adventures and step back, even if only briefly with friends, all over again.

Those who laugh with us will also be alongside us during the worst days.

Count on it.

HAZE

As quickly as a light switch turning on impacts a dark room, everything changed in our premature delivery process. There was a new tone in the doctor's voice—one which hadn't done anything to keep my nerves at ease.

She was now sternly businesslike, direct, and very commanding. Hearing her voice like this instead of the one used at the initial greeting was a stark contrast. She was now very serious about what she needed to do next.

I couldn't figure out what the demand was for; she needed *something* and needed it immediately!

She repeated the request a second time, louder than the first one.

Behind the draped curtain, your imagination tends to work against you as it allows a magnification for every little detail. You can hear whispers and monotone talking but without any color added to them to decipher fully what is going down.

When such a loud, forceful statement is made, it can shake you. Not trying to think the worst, her voice and rapid succession of wording made it difficult not to worry. Whatever happened here was no longer the typical walk-in-the-park procedure she must have performed on hundreds of other occasions.

The urgency in voices raced against time based on whatever was causing his sudden critical condition. Sitting there, I could hear stuff going down behind that drapery but couldn't see a damn thing to help myself make sense of things. Machines were cranking, movements were pronounced, and the frequent squeaking of shoes on the floor told me there was a ton of back-and-forth action.

What was clear were the rapid actions being taken and the now apparent rhythmic breathing in and out from the delivery doctor. In and out, she was forcing air. She sounded like she had just run up a few flights of stairs.

Was I listening to her feverishly trying to save a baby born lifeless?

Were these the final moments of his battle playing out before us on the other side of the curtain?

Could it be his soul was about to drift out from within and rise from whatever excuse of an unformed body he may have been cursed to possess?

What the hell is going on?

There were no answers to any of these questions coming our way. It was almost like we were stuck in some suspended animation.

First, there was that sudden rush of commotion, and now it was all over without us receiving any updates. I had no idea if the baby was even back there or if he had already been taken away.

I'm not sure I could have imagined any sound richer to hear than Kaden making it known that he was ready to meet us. I quickly prayed to God that we might be blessed to listen to him, even if only for a moment.

It never happened.

There was no opportunity for a quick look or gentle touching graze with our son—they were fervently trying to save him as soon as he came out. We never even saw Kaden, as he was taken from the womb and given false life via technology by rushing him away in milliseconds to keep his heart beating, his lungs expanding, and making every other effort to keep him alive.

Spending any time with a baby such as ours isn't immediately possible when your organs aren't working on their own. Kaden needed to be hooked immediately to machines, so any formal introductions must wait. We could only take their word that a baby boy was delivered.

I had no idea if he was born dead and they were trying to revive him or if he was still conscious and they were saving him. Everything was left in the air as it all went down that quickly.

Was it a mercy effort not to communicate for fear of falsely raising our hopes? In reality, it was all still playing out, I guess.

They hadn't told us anything further about his condition other than, "They were working on him."

Stacey was stitched up and taken into another room for recovery and observation. She was looped out and mostly unaware of the situation and the urgency on display.

With hospital scrubs still on, I gathered what may have been left of my composure, unsure what to tell family, and headed to the cafeteria area to update the others. They needed information, but what the hell would I share with them?

The drizzle continued outside, and the raindrops taunted me as I walked across the open-air court toward the two glass doors before me. My mother, mother-in-law, and Stacey's best friend were waiting for information. I knew there wasn't much to say to them, but any words at all were better than having them wait longer for small information nuggets to come their way.

They looked so intently at me that it was almost as if they were already pre-expecting to hear the worst news possible. Eyes red, watery, concerned stares—the works.

Maybe the rationale was to be on guard emotionally and then let it down should things not be as dire. I had never seen the same look of concern on three faces simultaneously, whatever their plans were. They were crying as they stared at every word formed by my lips. It was as if none had taken a full breath for hours. One way or another, my presence signified that it was time to inhale again.

First, I assured Stacey's mom that she was resting and in recovery. There was no way I could even know her condition at that exact time, either, so I made some assumptions. I had zero worries about her physical state; the emotional side was up in the air until we had more clarity. Since there were no visible signs of duress with her during the delivery, it felt safe to assume all would be alright with her.

By this knowledge share, I was halfway there, providing some modicum of calm by passing on the few delivery room details I had. Truthfully, there was not much to be done to assuage the circumstance when you are talking haphazardly about the status of a baby removed from the womb three months early.

What I said next were the only four words that came to mind. They made sense in a flabbergasted way regarding Kaden. "He was born alive."

I spoke with noticeable uncertainty because my intent was genuine.

They rattled from my tongue and came out of me almost incredulously. I had nothing more to offer; there hadn't been time for me to even consider what I felt.

Like a soldier returning from the battlefield, my legs slowly taxied me back to our hospital room to regain my composure and consider the event entirely.

What the hell had just happened?

This morning had all gone down so confusingly; the previous minutes and hours needed to be sorted and organized correctly.

Being alone now allowed me to plan how to comfort Stacey if bad news followed later— to figure out how to quickly put myself in a strong enough emotional place to be there for her. There was time for a quick cry if it happened suddenly for me.

Had his status changed since walking over to meet with them or on my way back to the room?

I kept sorting the possibilities of what was taking place, hoping to find some obvious answers that weren't there yet.

At a time of critical adversity, we must fully process our emotions. Closing my eyes, I captured a few quiet moments to figure out where my head was. Appropriately, this short time alone was exactly what I needed, but it was also one of the worst things I might have done.

The rain continued outside as the rest of the world moved along predictably. Alone in the room, I stared at what portion of the sky I could see.

How and where was baby Kaden?

Alone, I repeatedly tried to convince myself—shaking my head back and forth in a hazy state of rationalization—that everything was going to be okay.

There is no way our son could leave us now after being born alive.

No damn way.

FIFTH INNING

* * *

TEN

My description of Kaden here seems overdramatized. It might never become believable until you experience firsthand what it is like to have a child born as prematurely as he was, the tiniest human being I have ever cast my eyes upon.

Children are not supposed to be born looking like he did. In truth, he was hard to visit. He was my son, and as much as I loved everything about him, his sight was not easy to accept. Visually, the overwhelm was instantly powerful.

These chapters are all brought back from time as accurately to yesterday as possible. There were no plans for crafting any books back then, but I knew this part of our family journey was unique and needed to be captured, so I wrote down everything. Thankfully, the treasure trove of notes and scribbling I did each day allows me to share this with you as close to how it was experienced.

The information here is accurate, and nothing has been fabricated for effect. One thing is always sure: I don't take embellishment liberties when I write. You get my honest storytelling. I don't believe there is any other way than to be fully transparent.

After what we had gone through in Aryn's journey, I viewed prematurity differently, but this experience opened my eyes to so much more. The first time I saw "K" was somewhat perplexing.

Before walking to the NICU, I had no idea what a baby delivered so early would look like. I'm still unsure if I was more amazed, unnerved, or a combination of both. Perhaps it was slightly numbing, too.

Grand expectations can be our most significant obstacles to resolve. After we set them in place, if not met, the weight can loom large and be, at times, harmful. If they remain unaltered or revised, they can ruin a day, a week, a month, or even a lifetime. I have learned to temper mine now, but this learning process truly began the first time I was blessed to see this baby.

There are also routine expectations that require little thought because they are very predictable in most cases. They have nothing to do with the obvious side of becoming a human but are more on the apparent side of consistency in becoming one—if that makes any sense. We expect each of us to have a head, arms, legs, torso, and the ability to perform advanced, rational thoughts. The aggregate is the human form.

Another basic example is when you travel to a zoo to see the zebras; you already know you will see a horse with black and white stripes. No surprises, no big deal. We have all seen them many times.

We accept grass to be green and blood to be red. It is how certain things are taught to us as always being the case. Carrots are orange, long, and round. The list of examples goes on and on.

And then there are some exceptions, too.

Somewhere between my expectation as a parent to give my child the perfect body and my casual glance down and seeing a typical newborn with the size, colorings, and behaviors of one, there Kaden was.

He resided toward the middle left of the NICU, demanding most of the attention there. It was almost confusing to approach this abnormally tremendous amount of equipment surrounding such a small patch of life. He was not visible unless you walked over and looked directly down into his crib.

K weighed twenty ounces at birth. He was a mere two-thirds of the original estimate given to us earlier in the week before delivery. He was also four pounds lighter than the birth weight of his prematurely delivered older brother.

Back then, we thought Aryn was small! This second baby of ours was breaking all the rules.

Nothing about him was as expected. Kaden wasn't like anything imaginable; he was pretty unimaginable. Visually, it wasn't calming at all. I won't lie here to massage the truth. I never want to see another human born that size. It simply isn't natural.

When I say he was little, I'm talking about a "'holy cow" moment here. Truthfully, my hand could have covered his entire body, keeping him hidden from sight altogether.

His general size was that of a toy. To describe him easily, one could compare his overall appearance to one of those tiny medical dolls from the sixties and seventies. These dolls let you see right through the skin, exposing veins, arteries, and muscles. He looked like one of those, but not quite as big. Yes, I said that.

Kaden didn't look like a baby; more like a tiny hamster hooked up to a multitude of equipment, making the entire spectacle much more unique.

When I was a little boy a hundred years back, my guinea pig lived in a small, box-type structure in my bedroom. While it sounds weird to draw a parallel here, I was reminded of this. Kaden wasn't much bigger, if at all. He was probably smaller. His sleeping enclosure was similar in size to what my pet had called home.

His frame was about the circumference of half a candle, one sitting on the table during the holidays. Even in this description, I am being generous. Because everything was so noticeably covered up, it was challenging to determine if he was even proportionate.

Our son was not longer than the length of a TV remote control. Similar to the one I had put down earlier in Stacey's hospital room before coming to see him.

His color was a brownish hue, not the typical pinkish color you would expect. I can't even describe it accurately because it was almost like his skin was a cross between see-through and an utterly unique pigment.

There were also many red blotches around his torso, adding something different. Not knowing what they were, I could only assume they were formed naturally for some reason, considering his condition. Maybe they were a reaction from those steroids.

A person who suddenly loses a tremendous amount of weight often has an excess bulk of stretchy skin with no area to occupy anymore. Since Kaden did not have much body mass in the first place, his skin was extremely loose. It seemed content to hang off, void of any real purpose.

Funnily, it looked like it had been planning on covering much more of an area to work with. Since he was born so early, suddenly, he, too, was left with an excess of it. In this case, he hadn't lost weight at all. He hadn't gained it yet. It was just the opposite of extreme pound-shedding!

At first, it was a challenge to discover his eye color, as they seemingly never opened. I'm not confident he had the strength to do so, nor can I recall how long it took until I saw them open. He was always sleeping.

Kaden's walnut head often remained unmoved for hours, tilted off to the side as if it was no more significant than a harvest nut in a bowl at Thanksgiving. He didn't have the strength in his neck yet. His face was covered in what I can only explain as being like soft fuzz found around the circumference of a ripe peach.

His fingers were so stubby that you could not even hold them, and he did not have functioning hands yet. It was too much for him to even attempt to grasp at anything. They were there but barely usable. Due to their size, they were merely ornamental.

When I collectively placed all five of those minuscule digits together, they couldn't even cover up the end of my pinky finger. I'm not sure there was room for nails to begin growing, let alone much in terms of bone formation yet.

His underdeveloped legs stuck out from his diaper and appeared to be just two micro-sized, semi-elongated bundles of stretchy tissue. There were bones holding him together, but they couldn't have been solid. I can't even imagine how small they were inside his two limbs.

For some additional unique perspective, I slid my wedding band off at one point, past his foot and ankle, and up his leg to his crotch. It glided all the way up without any trouble at all. Incredibly, my ring was larger than his entire thigh circumference.

Somewhere, there is a picture of this. Because it was so unbelievable, I made it my mission to capture this disparity visually.

The feet each measured just under an inch long if that. Again, for scale and scope purposes, when we placed two dimes side by side, they covered up the footprint on his birth card. (See the picture at the end of the chapter for reference.)

I had never seen diapers so tiny, either.

Imagine one fitting comfortably on your cell phone, pretending it was human. Even placed as tightly as possible on him, unbelievably, these still slid off easily. They resembled an article that might fit perfectly on a child's doll, and still, they were too big for our son.

He never had any clothes to wear for a long time, except for those diapers. Aside from toy clothes, they aren't made small enough to fit a baby weighing only a pound. (He lost weight in there.)

Think about that.

Even the simplest gestures become a burden when born this size. One thing that struck me as odd was that he was always eerily still, rarely moving. It concerned me, incredibly so, to stand and look down at an utterly motionless life. There was not enough energy within him even to flinch.

One might have jumped to horrible conclusions without checking the monitors to know he was okay.

When it came to Kaden, I think the phrase for his first days of life had to have been, "Oh *my gosh!*"

Typically, when those words came out, they were followed quickly by a head shake and then a deliberate nervous hand brushing through hair across the top of the head from front to back. Again, there is absolutely nothing natural about viewing a human being Kaden's size.

When the family was eventually allowed to visit, we warned them about what they would experience. Words only do so much; every person reacts according to their shock tolerance.

Predictably, most were initially confident and sure of themselves in the washing and prep rooms. Still, as soon as they approached and placed their eyes on our son, their facade was entirely wiped away.

To conclude, our son was a tender human mass of undeveloped organs and tissues that had previously joined to form life and co-exist. Now, three months before having the normal development progression to do so, all was suddenly interrupted, leaving an unfinished body to find a way to become fit for sustaining life.

There is no other way for me to put it.

KADEN

BRIGHAM AND WOMEN'S HOSPITAL

My Name **Morrison**

My Parents' Names Stacey - Aric

Birthdate 5.5.06   Time 9³²   Weight 1 lb 4 oz   G.A. 28 6/7

My Private Pediatrician Rushaurd Krabel   Ph # 617.923.1040

My COMMUNITY HOSPITAL _____

My Primary Doctor _____

My Primary Nurse Laura Hoyt Christina Meehan

Mari Silva Izzy   Chris O.

Deanna B Friend

ARTIFICIAL

Our son was being kept alive by technology and only technology.

Stacks upon stacks of blinking, lighted medical fixtures were positioned everywhere, forming a horseshoe pattern around what appeared to be a high-tech, new-age sleeping space. It was a sealed-off, incubated type of germ-free, sterile container bed not unlike the one his brother had first lived in upon his birth.

The machines surrounding Kaden were performing tasks to keep his organs functioning correctly until the day came that each might do so independently. It was unnatural to witness such a display, knowing that human life lay utterly dependent on this excess of technology. But there he was, doing his best to adapt.

From even a close distance, tubes of various sizes and shapes, medication drips, and contacts appeared to float on air inside the incubator bed. You could barely see his extremities, let alone a torso and limbs, where all this stuff was attached. Despite those invasive things sticking out from him, he looked at peace amidst this artificial electronic forest of modified plastic and rubber.

Both arms were heavily linked with wires when you could even make them out. He had monitors attached to both legs, as it looked like every possible part was connected to something for some medical reason. There was so much activity in IVs that it was hard to figure out where it came from or which display it was connected to.

This incredible interstate of lines and tubes assisted his underdeveloped and non-functioning body to do things they were utterly incapable of alone. There was barely anything working on its own within him yet.

One of these tubes and machines noticeably forced his lungs to inflate and breathe in succession. He had no independent breathing function, so an endotracheal tube in his throat past his vocal apparatus did the work. It was in place to allow the airway to remain clear for the appropriate oxygen and carbon dioxide exchange. Poor K would be committed to this thick, rubber reality until he could finally breathe independently. It didn't look enjoyable.

How uncomfortable it is to exist there with a big, circular thing sticking up and out of your mouth.

It remained for months. Imagine existing with a tube coming from down your throat and out your mouth to a machine that ultimately kept you alive. One of my most enormous wishes then was for the day to arrive when he could breathe via two strong, independent, self-pumping lungs and be off that terrible-looking rubber curse of a pipe.

You could barely even see his chest expand, let alone tell it was a human being in there. When I say there was no discernable midsection, take it for what it is.

It is hard to process how something so fragile and nonfunctioning could have survived birth, let alone been kept alive by these machines. Although K was proof it was possible, I never would have believed it had I not witnessed this through my own eyes. I now better understand how crucial it was for them in that delivery room.

When Aryn finally came to the hospital to meet his brother for the first time, he commented that Kaden looked like a "squirrel."

In true fashion for a kid his age, he was more concerned with making sure his brother had a penis than his being threatened by all those intimidating machines keeping him alive. We laughed together as he sought this validation from his great-grandmother Helen in the waiting room afterward.

He was also relieved to know that it worked okay.

Upon a glance down, if they were close enough to do so, it instantly became known to everyone that here was a unique sight to behold. Kaden's size put the other premature babies to shame! Comparatively speaking, they were giants.

Many other families walked by, thinking he was an empty bed surrounded by machines.

Seeing this all put his incapable state into perspective. He wasn't thriving in any way but barely surviving. There were no guarantees that the next day might not be his last. It was that uncertain. Each second of every hour was all we had. While there, neither of us gave a crap about *tomorrow* with him; we could only live in the moment.

Kaden was struggling to make it.

If he did, the doctors would all be right in their previous assumptions. Our son was going to face significant challenges in the future. How could he not?

Very few pictures of K exist from back then. Only a handful were taken between us; it didn't seem appropriate. Somehow, capturing a still image of a human being born so early and kept alive by machinery wasn't suitable. It felt almost exploitative.

If you visit the NICU in a hospital, you will not leave as the same person who entered. It's a place to force you to look at life differently. Nothing externally matters if your existence comes down to solely relying upon the aid of machines to keep you alive.

Being the parent to a baby born under this kind of dependency, suddenly, the only thing that does is to preserve life artificially.

To hell with anything else.

STITCHES

Imagine building a house using only plastic on the outer walls, half the electrical system installed, the pipes not flowing water, and a furnace that is only half connected. Then, walking up to the new homeowner and handing them the keys. There is still so much work to do to make it habitable, which will take much longer.

You may also expect parts of the building job to require some rework, such as correcting defective products. Rushing a process always has risks.

This crude scenario is one that I draw a parallel to with Kaden.

It was a relief to discover no signs that our baby had Down syndrome, spina bifida, or blindness. There was still so much more to be worried about, but at least this was conclusive information. Nothing else could be yet determined and would only play out over time.

It is relieving to check off these boxes for peace of mind, but when you create a human life the size of a banana, there is much more to come, including developmental corrections involving surgery.

When I think about it, Kaden was more like the size of a minor, plastic water container a person drinks casually while working out in the gym. Rarely is any thought given to what size it is. If we laid one next to him, both would be identical in length and girth.

The only touching allowed was via gloves attached to his crib structure, the same kind we had used with Aryn five years earlier. You had to reach in through them as there was no skin contact, but at least it was something.

Kaden wasn't taken out of the crib at all, so there weren't many reasons to reach in with rubber fingers except maybe to poke at the cute little guy and hope for a smile or to change him. It sure would have been nice to cradle our son, but with all that equipment hooked up, it wasn't possible for quite some time.

Thankfully, everything seemed to be in place from a physical attribute perspective regarding missing limbs or digits. All appendages appeared proportionate, and we could enjoy a huge exhale of relief.

There was an exception: One of his legs was longer than the other. Generally speaking, this was no big deal when you consider the entirety of his condition compared to all the physical deformities we had been warned about. He might have a limp or walk with a gait; we surmised it would add more to his individuality and make him unique and special—because he was.

Kaden was also born with a severe physical defect discovered soon after birth. They had told us it was not uncommon for premature babies to be born with this one, but it didn't make accepting it any easier at first. When your son is being discussed in the same breath as having a hole in a part of his tiny heart, you immediately become in tune with what it means: a timely operation.

Amazingly, surgery on a baby not even seven days old didn't weigh as heavily on our alarm scale as you might think. We were so happy to have our child with us after such a crazy pregnancy; anything new from there became a compartmentalized concern. This was a serious issue, but it paled compared to what we had already been through over the previous week.

Can you say house money?

Today, if you told me my child needed to have a critically dangerous operation, I'd throw my hands up and freak out. Anxiety would return and welcome the opportunity to kick my butt.

Back then, inner exhaustion demanded we reprioritize our stressors. In addition, he had already been operated on one other time. Oddly, maybe we expected him to have a few of these kinds of procedures since his body was less than perfect, medically speaking. Whatever was causing our modified sense of bravado, it kept us both at bay.

On the day of the aortic repair operation, I sat at lunch with two coworkers at a restaurant in Somerville, just east of the city. It was a typical meeting, with light conversation overtaking most of it. I was as happy to be out of the hospital for two hours as I was to be with them. The casual talk was welcome, and my objective was not to disclose any recent drama in my life but merely to attempt to escape.

Unfortunately, my son's status still became a more significant part of our dialogue since his birth had been so recent. While giving them the briefest update possible to avoid talking about it, I casually mentioned that he was having open heart surgery taking place while we were meeting.

Instantly, you would have thought I had divulged some incredible bombshell secret hidden from the world for centuries.

The guys in my party stopped eating and drinking, collectively opened their mouths, and stared at me while trying to process what they had just heard.

"Why the hell was I sitting there with them instead of with my wife waiting?"

The realization that I was with them rather than being at the hospital waiting for Kaden to come out of surgery was mindblowing to both. To an outsider, I get it, but as the guy experiencing this ordeal, there were profound reasons for my being with them instead. You had to be in my shoes to understand my reasoning fully.

Even now, I would do the same thing all over again. You have to get away sometimes to remain spiritually whole. My days of tap dancing on eggshells needed a rest.

Kaden's overall condition was precarious because he was so small and so reliant upon those stacks of machines all around him. Still, somehow, we both had gained inner confidence in his ability to pull through whatever else might come his way. Because he survived the birth, that alone was our accurate benchmark. Everything else would be taken a little more lightly in stride.

Maybe when you've already gone through so much heavy stuff, you trick yourself into thinking certain things will automatically turn out okay. When facing long stretches of adversity, as humans, we evolve and reprioritize our triggers and stressors. It just happens.

The aortic correction was performed by entering through his left side with a small incision in his back. Based on his scar, the dimension wasn't much. I was surprised they entered him this way instead of through his chest. His heart couldn't have been easy to repair because it was so damn small, let alone navigate a way to even get to it.

How does one even operate on a one-pound baby in the first place? Those tools must have been unique to perform such delicate work. Who makes these instruments, and how extensive is their customer base? It is all quite fascinating.

By the time I returned to the hospital, Kaden was in recovery, and Stacey was quietly waiting for him to come out. He pulled through with flying colors, as we knew he would.

Unfortunately, this was not the only procedure K underwent during those initial two years of his life. It was merely the second in a long and detailed series to come. None were as serious as repairing a hole in an aortic valve, but they were all still essential as he quickly became as familiar with the operating room as we did with the waiting room.

Open-heart surgery on a one-week-old sixteen-ounce human being.

Just another day for the Morrison family.

HOMESICK

SATURDAY, SEPTEMBER, 23, 2006

There are occasions when the trappings of circumstance become all too real. When you drop off your little boy daily to the same question, "Is my baby brother coming home today?" it destroys you.

How long can you keep a young child waiting?

I found myself letting Aryn down day after day and, in doing so, crushing his hope for change. Most of the time, I was the one to drive him to school or daycare in the morning, and hearing him say this always affected me. It is a long time for a little boy to wait for his new baby brother to arrive. He wanted to play with him, love him, and show him off to his school pals.

Our circumstance became complicated when he could not understand the complexities of why his baby brother had never been able to sleep in his bed, in his room, or in our own house. Nothing could be done to speed up the process; only time, medicine, and technology could fix our son. Essentially, we existed all spring and summer without all living together.

Poor Aryn was thrown for a loop, not having us both there.

Though my opinion has evolved somewhat, the concept of a family not being complete until all members exist under one roof still holds. On paper, we were a family of four, but it wasn't official yet.

For almost half a year, we lived in two separate worlds. You might say we were a divided family purely due to our situation and not by choice. We each had a child to take care of. One of us was always away in Boston with Kaden, while the other kept up the Peterborough consistency for Aryn.

My mother wrote a welcome message on our dry-erase board in the kitchen to help ratchet up the anticipation for Kaden's final arrival home. Seventeen years later, it remains carefully preserved and untouched as a reminder of this special day.

Aryn sat in the living room window that Saturday and continued asking his nana when we were arriving with his baby brother in tow. He was out of his mind excited to finally have Kaden come home that afternoon to live with us as the newest member of the Morrison family.

This was a big day for him. As we all did, he needed to heal. Tonight, he would sleep in his crib, room, and our wonderful, newly built home.

Unfortunately, Aryn suffered the most during his childhood; he was too young to realize it, but to this day, I know many of these years linger unreconciled within him. For almost six months, he hadn't been able to experience both of his parents sleeping under the same roof as it had always been before his brother was born. We were aware nothing about this was wholesome. We had become a short-term, broken home.

I captured the day on video as Aryn ran down the walkway toward the car to greet his brother and welcome him home for the first time. It was beyond describable how happy he was to have everyone there.

On the first evening with K, I took a few minutes to reflect again, considering how far we had traveled as a family. Our boys had covered some severe medical ground in the past seven years. I was experiencing deeper feelings within myself as I reviewed our timeline for all these memories while seeking peace.

We made it through, were together, and were on the verge of new beginnings. It was nice to feel like it might all be put away now; time to move on. Hopefully, all that madness was going to be over for a long, long time.

There were going to be some more issues concerning Kaden, but by far and large, the rest of the challenges might remain away from us for a while.

A fake log flame danced casually in the fireplace, providing movement in the background as I sat in the living room listening to specially selected songs containing deep meaning.

We prepared for the worst that February as I prayed to the heavens every evening before bed for it not to happen. Many nights, I fell asleep without believing that things would be okay. It felt like the deck had been stacked somehow, and the hand was about to be lost at any time.

The instances of tensing up suddenly as teams rushed into the NICU to assist him were also put behind us. There were so many nights that Kaden had taken a turn; when our phone rang after hours, we knew it wasn't from the doctors wanting to share happy news about Kaden.

All those trips back and forth to the hospital ended on this day, too. Those various impromptu visits were now somewhat over. The numerous overnight phone calls requesting the other parent come to Boston immediately were also over.

Kaden was home. One hundred forty-one days after his birth, on September 23, 2006, he was finally ours to keep.

While sitting in the same room, in the same chair that I searched for his name that evening back on May 4, the circle was complete. I sipped on what may have been the best glass of white wine I had ever enjoyed in my entire life.

Around eleven p.m., I turned the lights off downstairs one by one and relaxed by the fire for a few more minutes alone. There was no stress, anxiety, or immediate worries to speak of—a scarce time for me.

Kaden was unique; what was in store for us was unknown. None of this was worth thinking about. Why bother?

As I passed Aryn's room, I whispered, "Goodnight, pal." As usual, his milk cup with the sippy straw and zoo-themed snack plate remained on his bed stand.

His deliberate breathing assured me he was happily in slumber, probably for the first time in a long while.

Across the hall, I walked into K's room and looked down into the crib to witness him in there for his first night home. It felt weird to see this, but still, it was the best experience ever—something we had visualized for almost a year.

On the next page is a picture of a Christmas gift I gave Stacey that year, displaying the coins held in my pocket for all those days.

She never knew they existed.

I reached into my right backside pocket, collected those same two lucky pennies from my jeans, and gently placed both heads-up on the nightstand one last time for safekeeping.

They weren't needed anymore.

"You and I rushed back to the hospital.
We were given abysmal odds.
In the parking lot outside
I found two pennies – heads-up.
Those pennies stayed with me.
for luck through the birth of our son
until he arrived home.
In your possession now,
are the two luckiest pennies
in the world."

12/25/2006

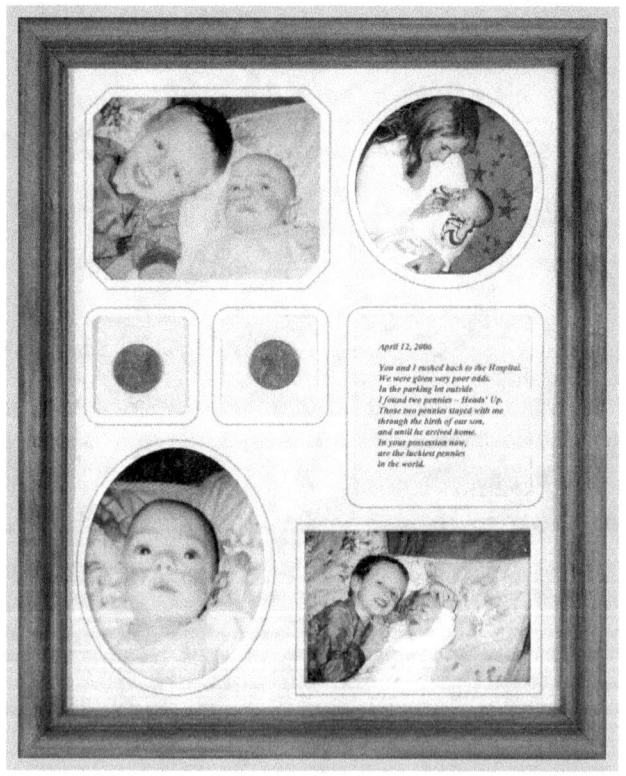

SIXTH INNING

* * *

GREEN

You now have a semi-decent picture of Kaden from a physical and developmental perspective. It would be wrong for me not to mention one unique attribute that innocently and tenderly encapsulates this entire early journey.

To this day, I have a piece of molded rubber carefully preserved as a poignant reminder of what it once represented: a source of comfort to Kaden during his first few years. Like his passive demeanor, his light green binkie also beautifully represented our son. From early on, this item morphed into his identity or trademark, if such a thing exists for a child barely twelve months old.

Back then, he was rarely seen without it constantly in his mouth. It was as much a part of him as his arms, legs, eyes, or ears. When you saw Kaden, you saw green rubber too.

He did the cutest thing with it, which, in many ways, became as much of his unique identity as any physical part of him. He had a repetitive pattern of giving it a few hearty sucks every minute or so and then allowing it to remain there in place until the next round began all over again. It rarely fell out, so he had perfected a way to keep it in place without sucking.

This simple, formed piece of rubber comforted him as much as a blanket or stuffed animal. It was there in place from morning to night, ready for a few quick sucks. Even at bedtime, it remained in his mouth until he fell asleep, and it dropped out. Kaden would be sound asleep, and we always knew somewhere close to his head on the bed would also be the green binkie.

When he was aggressive or restless, nine times out of ten, it was because the pinkie was not readily available. This was Kaden.

His second year of life was a steady regimen of medical ordeals, but nothing close to what I would consider significant compared to some of the other crap we had faced. There were still many challenges with him regularly, which required us to go back and forth for subsequent procedures and further testing. The biggest was his digestive regurgitation.

Kaden was placed on a special liquid to aid his physical growth because he was born so small—his unfortunate drinking pattern was very predictable in a messy way. His input was regularly given as it should have been, regarding appetite during every single feed, without fail, but he couldn't keep it all down.

We always placed a towel across the front of him during his bottle sessions because shortly after, he would cough a few times and throw the formula up all down the front of himself. Within seconds, we could count on his entire chin, neck, chest, and belly to become soaked with the same bottle feed.

We went through our fair share of outfits and towels during this period.

Meals quickly became a race against time. We kept our fingers crossed, hoping he might retain some of his bottles, but for the most part, more often than not, it all came back up, causing him to be dangerously close to malnourished. Medically and physically, something was wrong with him.

This behavior was not some random act. It was a regular occurrence during every meal, as he never kept it inside for long. This was a tremendous problem because he was already fragile. Not getting enough calories and nourishment only compounded his already complex condition. Kaden was most often on his back or cradled in a lap, so careful attention needed to be paid at all times. He could not sit up; there was also a constant choking hazard here.

To remedy this temporarily, until they were able to discover what was causing him to vomit, the doctors eventually cut him open again for the umpteenth time. They placed a feeding tube into his belly for a temporary solution. We didn't want to do it, but it happened more out of desperation because this issue impacted his overall health.

Instead of traditional meals going through his mouth, this device bypassed the need to swallow. It was a hole created right through his skin, directly into his stomach. His g-tube consisted of a small, button-like apparatus called a mickey, which protruded from the side of his stomach.

It was held with a rubber, balloon-like device filled with water to keep it within the cavity at all times. When feeding, we attached a syringe to the button; gravity did its thing, and liquid calories drained directly through a small tube into his belly. There was no more messy upchucking to speak of, but it took time to drain and required extra bags of equipment to be lugged around all the time

—a pain in the ass.

At night, we hooked it up to a machine hanging off the side of his crib, automatically administering his bottle feed via a timing schedule through a long, thin tube. More equipment for us carry. It hung off his stroller or bouncy seat when napping, continuing the flow directly into him.

There was blood, pus, oozing, and a bright red ring around the opening—disturbing to see if you aren't prepared in advance. This all required cleanup and regular maintenance to keep it from getting infected. Despite having to look at this nasty, gaping opening all the time, we quickly got over it and adjusted.

In short, it was a patch job until we could find more answers. Having a baby with a tube sticking out of his stomach wasn't perfect, but it bypassed the issue in the bigger picture. His condition wasn't likely to go away independently, which meant putting him through many uncomfortable tests.

Regular hospital visits remained a large part of our lives for the balance of 2006 and the first part of 2007. Some were relatively routine, and some were more involved, requiring extended stays. On average, our family unit was still apart for long stretches, and we desperately needed to find some consistent structure to keep us all whole.

Between Aryn's young needs, Kaden's medical ordeals, and my constantly demanding work schedule, there always seemed to be more than a few balls up in the air.

It might have been nice to let them all fall just once.

CUT

We learned within that first year that K's hearing was severely restricted in his right ear while the left appeared completely fine. This one was functioning at an almost deaf level. They told us he had, at best, around 10-15% capability, which made some sense as Kaden tended to favor turning his head to one side to listen.

We considered allowing them to operate and examine what might be happening, but we saw no crucial reason to cause him any more pain by invasive manipulation. He had already been through a lot. Hearing loss would be addressed later after his more pressing issues were rectified. We both agreed that when Kaden hit a certain age, an aid would do just fine to compensate.

Those units are now so small that it wouldn't even be a concern for any vanity reasons as he grew up. It was no big deal for us to accept; it was what it was. They warned us about this before his birth, so it wasn't that much of a surprise either. Life-threatening issues mattered, not a hearing deficiency.

He had his limbs, functioning organs, a repaired heart, and a recently installed feeding tube. It was all good as he progressed a little more each month.

Because Kaden had been under medical care for fourteen months, I can honestly say that consistency in our family unit was still sorely lacking, even after he had been home for a while. I had been optimistic that we would find a way to work together in terms of synergy, but truthfully, it still hadn't been possible.

Stacey and I were burnt out physically and emotionally. We all needed to start over in one way or another, as we had been waiting for things to settle down every year since our marriage.

Since she was home all day that summer caring for Kaden and his continuous medical idiosyncrasies, an opportunity to purchase a cottage at the ocean became available, so we pounced on it. Being in Maine was much more fun than being in the woods alone with squirrels and the occasional goat from next door.

How great to put all the madness behind us and enjoy family time on the beach. Kaden was hooked up to an oxygen tank and nasal cannula, which added a unique dimension to transporting him to the sand, but we kept him covered and made it work. He wasn't walking, so a crib on the beach was still the only option. The Morrison's, a family of four with a unique background, tried to blend in.

We were noticeable when approaching. If you ever saw us coming, it would be obvious who we were with all of our oxygen, tubes, bags, and other medical necessities in tow.

It was refreshingly wonderful to do events together as a complete family for a change, like going to the park or attending baseball games—two adults in the front seat and two kids in the back. As

Sundays came around, we also retook day trips as a family, like we used to do with Aryn.

In addition, we began having movie nights with pizza and snacks or taking trips to the local pond for swimming. We often brought the boys to the local community pool, too, where Aryn had swimming lessons.

In general, what we did never mattered; we were finally together, which alone was enough to create fulfillment. Indeed, it had been a very long and deserved time coming.

The front yard of our place in Peterborough had the most perfectly manicured green grass of any other house in the neighborhood. It was a plush lawn that made the property stand out, not in an arrogant way, but in one that made you feel good turning into the driveway. It was something I'd always wanted to have.

We owned a beautifully welcoming lot, so having the front yard represented well completed the picture. What is better than returning to a green, well-manicured property after a long day or week?

I've never been materialistic; effort on it wasn't for show; it was all about nourishing my frame of mind. Somehow, doing yard work was my way of trying hard to convince myself that things were on the upswing for us all—the end to all the running around constantly for medical appointments, too.

Each time I cut the grass, Aryn marched out and climbed onto my lap to ride the mower. It was so cute having him bounce around while we did an excellent job together cleaning up the yard for Mom and KK. Barely was there a Saturday that summer when the lawn wasn't cut by the two of us.

Quality time in its most basic form.

It is funny what you do with your kids to keep them entertained and smiling. To this day, my son still mentions those summer months when we sat together, buzzing around the yard—just the two of us sharing some father-son time in the most innocent way possible.

Maybe there is a lesson here:

• Amidst all the chaos, memories still have seeds to be planted for reaping tomorrow.

As parents, we forget in haste that our actions with children today can provide fortification for future flashbacks.

We often don't realize the impact some moments have on us as they occur.

Oh, to go back there again...

RODENT

We never considered the future with Kaden; we existed in the present. Looking ahead with him seemed unnecessary, but his constant medical trials forced us to think this way. As I mentioned before, there would be a long road ahead of us with him.

Everyone knew from very early on that Kaden was different because of his tiny size. By now, Aryn also understood that his brother was not like his other friends' siblings in many other ways. He had numerous complications that made him who he was.

He was not meant to be like any other. If he were, there might not be a story here.

His differences were no matter; he loved Kaden for the little toddler he was, always willing to do anything to support him. Watching them together was so lovely. Not in any way out of sympathy but purely out of love. He was always there alongside his smaller pal. Aryn was the best big brother on the planet, bar none.

Unsurprisingly, after living with rubber protruding from your mouth for almost six months, some long-term repercussions were caused. When an apparatus is attached to your body for an extended time, it will have an impact. While it was a relief to have that terrible thing gone, no one might have foreseen the permanent damage it did to our son. By now, it was noticeable.

The tubing ultimately caused paralysis to his vocal cords. They kept him alive by using the tube, but cost him something in doing so. I hated seeing it when it was stuck down his throat, and now the reminder of its damage would always live with us. Again, keeping things real here, this wasn't the most distressing reality for us to contend with.

At best, we were told he might have a high-pitched voice resembling a famous cartoon mouse—or the other extreme: Kaden was destined to be voiceless for his entire life. I figured that further down the road, perhaps he could use one of those mechanical voice boxes some people use if need be.

You begin to appreciate thinking about the bigger picture at this point in the game when your child is born the size of a cellphone, though. We honestly didn't concern ourselves about this one setback hardly at all. It wasn't worth it. So, his vocal cords were never going to function correctly, big deal. He could also learn sign language to communicate.

The unthought-of reality was that Kaden hadn't made any oral sounds since birth. First, there was that tube, and then there was paralysis. It was odd in one way but not so much in another way.

Our child was soundless.

You never heard if he cried (which was very rare). Nor did you enjoy an occasional hearty baby laugh or giggle. In one way, we missed out on these moments with him, but again, it was what it was. Kaden had gone through so much in his young existence.

Happiness to us had him home with the ability to breathe independently. He had that nasal cannula directly attached to an oxygen tank, but it was progress! As parents, you have to adjust to these conditions.

There, too, was another learning curve.

If you weren't with him to view his emotions, there was no way of knowing something was upsetting. The only way to learn was to see his face scrunch up in distress. It was impossible to stare at him constantly, so we always had to be mindful and keep as much of a watchful eye on him as was practical.

Monitors in his bedroom were useless at night; we could only listen to him breathing and occasionally moving around as best he could for such a weak, underdeveloped little guy. If he filled his diaper or was struggling, we needed to be well accustomed to listening for wrestling sounds in body movements instead of auditory cues.

We did have the option as he got a little older to correct this somewhat. He could have regular monthly injections for the rest of his natural life to aid his voice enough for it to be heard. The shot only lasted a short time, so returning to square one was bound to be the result again until the next one.

This didn't sound great to me, but we shelved it for future reference, just in case.

The other option for us was to accept that he wouldn't ever become a baritone singer and thus forgo a life of monthly needles in the future.

Through the years, I have learned to embrace perspective. I preach this concept regularly, regardless of how damaging a situation may appear. Instead of dwelling on the cost, I work on rejoicing in the benefit.

Considering how much else was wrong with Kaden, this new development could have been much worse. So, there would never be baby babble or cute word-forming utterances. For now, all was fine.

This part of Kaden wasn't meant to be; it was what made him *him*.

Plus, who isn't a big fan of that mouse anyway?

ROLL

Professionally, I was achieving much of what I had been striving for in terms of challenging myself more with every job role. Money flowed weekly as the constant trips, exclusive credentials, and elbow-rubbing with elites became my newest drug. Experiences were rolling towards me fast and hard, most of which people might dream of. I was very fortunate in this regard. We were not making our numbers, but the benefits of my job were undoubtedly pretty neat.

As mentioned before, while checking off these super-unique boxes was remarkably wonderful, the weight of what was going on back home sometimes counterbalanced any sense of accomplishment. That side of my life dissolved as soon as I entered my driveway.

My family challenges were another story.

Being the parent to a medically fragile child was slowly becoming much more complex than we could have imagined. While normalcy was still teasing us, it came and went like the tide. Some periods were acceptable and on track, while others quickly deteriorated into turmoil again.

By early 2008, Stacey and I were still knee-deep in the Hydrocephalus concerns with Aryn, and now, with Kaden, the developmental challenges became even more extensive as the early days went along. He was not catching up some two years after his birth. Comparatively speaking, K was the complete opposite of what we had seen regarding growth with Aryn. It hadn't taken a medical, psychological, or behavioral specialist to deduce that something cognitively might be wrong with our son.

Kaden didn't make any sounds, was very tiny, still had oxygen-assisted breathing, and generally appeared to be drifting farther away from *ordinary* in the traditional sense. The fact that he did not eat through the same conventional means as other children made it quite apparent that he was different from the rest. But there was so much more intellectually going on, or not.

For one, he regularly looked around without seeming to focus on anything. He stared at the ceiling, the walls, the floor, people, and anything else he found curious, appearing to be amazed at everything in many ways. His world was all about visual stimuli rather than wanting to touch, hold, or grab anything. He was happy to remain on his back for long stretches without attempting to roll, rock, or try something new.

Another noteworthy behavior was his constant shaking of his hands. It was never like an item could be picked up and looked at for some time. Kaden always had to shake it before tossing it back down almost immediately. His hands didn't function as they were supposed to; he was a flapper.

He was still unable to sit, stand up, crawl, or walk independently, nor was he displaying any signs of wanting to learn how. He was not performing the physical actions that a toddler his age should have been able to master. The best he could do was roll from side to side, clearly preferring to remain on his back instead. One charming attribute of his was his tendency to rest his right leg/foot over the other bent knee while on his back, as adults tend to do when sitting down.

He showed no interest in forming words either; faint grunting noises suited him just fine. This frustrated his big brother because Aryn wanted to play and talk with him like the other kids could with their siblings.

With Kaden, this was not happening.

Though very content in his world, he spent most of his time on the floor with a pillow under his head. Occasionally, we put him in a specially padded bouncy seat, which he liked very much because it kept him vertical. He was a mellow little guy who showed no desire to progress physically or intellectually. He laughed a lot and had an excellent demeanor for such an early medical case; he was mainly happy.

Kaden did enjoy bouncing up and down in the kitchen within a swing attached to a bunny-like cable. Often, he would jump around on that thing for long periods, up and down and back and forth, powered solely by his tiny feet. This activity was the sole extent of most of his mobility.

Finally, daily experiences with other children, such as playing in the grass, splashing in a pool, rolling balls, and placing things into his mouth, were all foreign to him. Kaden wanted no part in any of it. He was extremely passive and preferred to watch *Sesame Street* and *Barney* videos on television.

If our second son was developmentally challenged, those were all hints of trouble, almost confirming it. Like so much other stuff with K, we just rode with this, knowing it would all sort itself out. *One day at a time* was still our approach, and it worked well to keep us from being overcome with false possibilities.

To sum up, we didn't know precisely where we stood with him yet. Our son was unique in so many other ways. Each challenge with this child was his identity—nothing less.

On many occasions, I used to utter, "Just another chapter in the life of one Kaden Harding Morrison."

It was so damn appropriate.

SEVENTH INNING

* * *

CACTUS

WEDNESDAY, JANUARY 30, 2008

L iving in New England, if you weren't already, you almost needed to become a football fan, considering the team's historic run. Week after week, the New England Patriots marched along and dominated all competitors. It was a meteoric rise for the franchise that may never be equaled anytime soon, if ever again.

Come Sundays, the entire region was glued to a TV set to watch the team play. Their rising success had taken over the Northeast altogether.

Though Kaden had been on that feeding tube for most of his life, it did not address the ultimate reason why he could not eat food orally. It isn't normal to throw up everything immediately during consumption. After a year and a half of consumption through a feeding tube, we knew we still needed to address this for him.

The temporary fix served as a short solution to a more significant physical issue that had to be corrected: the esophagus and stomach were not working correctly. We found out that he was born with both of them malformed. Each was only partially formed, hence the constant reflux.

As we had been warned before his birth, there were going to be aspects of his physical body that might be at risk for normalcy. In addition to the others, we were aware of these two recently.

It all made perfect sense, but this reality also set another critical operation to be scheduled to correct this mess. The only resolution was to cut my son's upper abdomen open again.

This one was hard to accept because, this time, it wasn't as simple as going in and stitching up a tear or removing a small lump. Here, they wanted to manipulate his esophagus and stomach altogether. They needed to disconnect and reconnect them, changing the angle by repositioning each. Yikes!

For some of this, we discussed having a fundoplication on Kaden whereby the stomach is wrapped around the large intestine to reduce or prevent reflux recurrences. This was a very highly invasive and detailed procedure. What if it didn't work, or the reattachment of each wasn't being accepted property by his organs? Like so many other medical ordeals with Kaden, there were no guarantees with this one.

Might we be opening up another can of worms by taking him apart like this? I researched this operation online, which I probably should not have. It only magnified my stress. It was some serious stuff to perform this procedure. I wondered, too, what the long-term repercussions were when you move a stomach and esophagus around like two Checker pieces. Might it require many additional corrective surgeries?

It was rough to think about allowing them to again go inside our boy, who was a few months shy of two years old. Cutting open a toddler so repeatedly seemed cruel and unfair. We had no choice, though. Kaden had a tube sticking out of his stomach; we needed to remedy his condition.

The operation was scheduled for the following month in March, so it was constantly nagging at me in the back of my mind regardless of what else was happening in my day or week. It loomed on the near horizon like a storm cloud.

It is never about the first drop of rain or thunder crack. You know it will burst; the build-up and preparation for it to happen cause the most disruption.

On Wednesday, January 30th, 2008, my plane landed in Arizona as I was headed to see the Super Bowl and watch the Patriots play the New York Giants in the big game. As a benefit to my position, attending each year was a given. This one had more luster since the team had gone undefeated for the entire season. The opportunity for them to make history was looming, which added an entirely new dimension to the game.

I met Hall of Fame quarterback Steve Young early the morning before the game and talked with him. He was so very cool. Shortly after that, I was with Wes Welker from the Patriots. We then called my brother Pete and brother-in-law Peter for him to say "Hello" just for fun. They were both in Vegas for the game.

Attending the Super Bowl is the stuff of dreams for countless folks. It is easy to think being there would automatically distract anyone from whatever was going on in their life as it might instantly provide an escape from reality for about four blissful hours.

For most people, it would.

For me, it couldn't.

Unfortunately, even across the country in Scottsdale, Arizona, my team playing in the biggest game could not entirely remove my mind from Kaden. The upcoming operation he was scheduled to have in a few weeks still managed to command center stage within my skull. I hoped going on the trip might ease some of my worries. Knowing my child was again going to be sliced open in a matter of weeks was just too much for me to cast aside, even in the short term. Thank God for a never-ending supply of draft beers; they helped.

The Patriots ultimately lost the game that afternoon, and I received my fair share of razzing from my co-workers during the ride back in the chartered bus. It was all good, as we were a close bunch. No one knew of my mindset regarding Kaden; it was one of those things I hid well. Like so many other nuggets of information about my home life.

Suck it up, buttercup! Keep laughing, keep smiling, Aric. You've got this.

Maybe I missed my calling and should have been an actor instead.

We ventured to In and Out Burger shortly after the game, so the day wasn't a total loss for me. I could check that box off.

As luck would have it, I accidentally dumped my entire uneaten meal on the floor while walking to the table.

Stuff was everywhere as I scrambled to gather it and heave it into the trash can out of embarrassment and frustration. Then, I stood in the long, starved Super Bowl fan line all over again to reorder and pay for the same items for a second time—a fitting way to end the weekend.

It was my lot, I guess. Cryptic karma for being away from my family during such an unsettling time, leaving Stacey alone with Aryn and Kaden.

Our life was still a delicate medical mess.

TWILIGHT

Do you recall "The White Lady" from the first book in this series? We believe she had something to do with this.

On April 10, 2008, we traditionally celebrated Aryn's seventh and my forty-first birthday with cake, ice cream, and a few presents.

Roughly one week after this fun day, one of the most curious things I have ever experienced began to occur. You can draw your own opinions and conclusions from here.

There are so many swerves and turns in our story that it can be challenging to keep track, even for me—and I was there! We never told our families or anyone else about this. I am unsure why, but we didn't.

In our case, this overarching element quickly rose to the top and had to be included here. When I began gathering all the details that might have a place in this series, one aspect of our story was puzzling. I have my theories today, but I will never know the truth.

I believe when Kaden became very ill with a completely out-of-the-blue, dangerously high fever just a day before his scheduled corrective fundoplication procedure in March, there was an almost predetermined reason for it happening.

Kaden was absolutely fine every day during March leading up to this procedure. Now, less than twenty-four hours before they cut him open, like a switch being turned on by **Fate,** he became very ill. His fever spiked, and he became overcome with some mysterious ailment. His sudden turn caused that terrible operation to be put on hold.

It never did take place, either. I believe in my heart of hearts that his operation was destined *not* to occur. Somehow, that twist was interconnected with what happened in an otherworldly way. It made no sense back then, but it indeed does now.

This is where things suddenly became highly spooky.

A slight smirk often comes across people's lips when I tell this part of the story. They either think I have gone slightly mad or have spent too much time listening to Art Bell radio re-runs.

Throughout this chapter and two others, I tell these creepy details exactly as they happened. The information presented in the next few pages follows suit to introduce this phenomenon. If it helps sway your belief system, Stacey and I would gladly submit to a lie detector on this one!

All I can do is share it with you.

One night, I returned home from work to find Stacey standing in the baby's bedroom, quizzically looking around. I saw her positioned off to the side, getting ready to place her ear on the wall as though she wanted to listen in on a conversation.

There wasn't anyone in the next room to spy on.

She told me she had heard a strange buzzing sound earlier and couldn't figure out what had been causing it. According to her, it was a dullish, rather annoying sound. Not high-pitched or ear-piercing. It wasn't obnoxiously loud and haunting but prevalent enough to hear when it became known. It is best described quite simply as being a constant drone. The timing was void of any consistency or frequency. It could last for several continuous minutes or merely for a few seconds. The only predictable aspect of it was the sound of the noise itself.

I heard nothing after standing still, dismissing it as a toy running low on batteries in Aryn's room just across the hall. I never thought twice about it again.

It wasn't continuous initially and only happened briefly during the day. Since there was never any indication of when it would occur, the chance for both of us being home at the exact time it happened was pretty slim. These random noise instances became a joke between us. Stacey was regularly exposed to hearing the sound, but I never was.

Not even once.

When I came home from work at night, she told me about hearing the buzzing sound again. Marching up the stairs to Kaden's room, I stood there for a few minutes, listening for something that had only been rumored to have been confirmed. Then, after hearing absolutely nothing, I'd head back to the kitchen for dinner like a bonehead falling for a prank.

We repeated this exercise several times in one week. At this point, I began to think she was playing a joke on me. It was humorous watching me get off the couch, march up the stairs, and then stand aimlessly in the middle of our child's bedroom, hoping to hear some yet unidentifiable mysterious noise that may or may not even be real.

I had been getting a little portly from all the stress previously caused by K, but buy me a gym membership for Christmas instead of concocting some wild story to get me moving more. Don't make up some elaborate hoax to watch my fat ass go up and down the stairs several times each night!

It was as though I was on some hidden camera show where they kept gimmicking the person repeatedly. I climbed the stairs as if programmed to do so, like a monkey in a tree. The only thing I ever heard was my inner voice calling me a gullible jackass.

Another time, Stacey phoned me while I was in Rhode Island for work. She held it up from the middle of Kaden's room for me to verify that I, too, could hear it.

Like an idiot, I pressed the phone firmly against my ear, turning it all red, to witness...absolutely nothing. No strange sound came through the phone, yet she insisted on hearing it live while talking to me. Was my wife making this up?

Probably not.

In truth, I was convinced she was hearing something but casually dismissed it. Maybe it was caused by a motion-sensitive toy reacting to minor movement within the crib. If the buzzing noise wasn't keeping K awake or bothering him, so be it. We could eventually get to the bottom of the cause in due time.

The mysterious sound became a real cat-and-mouse game with Stacey, though. She wanted to find out once and for all what the heck it was.

It was as unpredictable as it was persistent and oddly taunting her.

Bigfoot, UFOs, The Loch Ness Monster, and other mysteries exist in our world. Now, there was another to add to the list.

At least in our home.

O J

It is incredible to see how fast time flies, but it is also odd how quickly long-gone details return so vividly with a minor amount of coaxing. On my drive home yesterday, I thought about one of them, and I decided it was essential to include it. You may find this nugget slightly bland in the general scheme of our story here, but because it played such a role back in the day, it felt important enough to mention.

For Kaden, as you may understand by now, needles and testing were not atypical during those first couple of years. Every time we took him in for what, on the surface, was a cough, rash, or primary annoyance, somehow, he also received another jab to the arm. This kid had more needles stuck into him by age two than many people do in an entire lifetime. No kidding.

Trips to the doctor's office were often met with concern from Aryn, always asking if K had received a shot that day. In the eyes of a five- or six-year-old, it might have just as well be akin to removing a limb.

The remainder of the evenings were usually filled by our oldest giving extra attention to ensure his younger brother was happy and comfortable after having endured such a traumatic experience. In the affirmative, his response was always, "Poor Kaden."

I will offer there is no more understanding, protective, and loving brother in the world.

He always had a caring heart, one of his many unique qualities. I am unsure if he related to medical trials because of his own from so early on or because seeing his brother so small and helpless in the NICU that first day affected him so dramatically. Either way, Aryn was always sympathetic, empathetic, and well-grounded regarding others' differences.

Medical assistance to support Kaden was so common at our house that Aryn learned to turn off the feeding equipment when the cycle was complete. Without giving it a second thought, he'd walk to the machine, press his tiny finger on the button, and shut it down—no big deal. He loved his new role and welcomed the chance to play a large part in helping his tiny sidekick grow stronger and develop. This was all a part of the job for a big brother.

In addition to helping out in these unique ways to care for his pal, Aryn was the first to discover that if you utter the phrase "Olivia Jane" to Kaden, it would immediately elicit his smile. At the beginning of one random evening, he came home and muttered it casually while sharing his day with us. Olivia Jane was the name of another child who attended the same after-school program as our son. I had never heard it mentioned before, but thankfully, it rolled out from his lips that night!

Upon hearing this the first time, Kaden immediately looked up and laughed, as only a two-year-old with paralyzed vocal cords could do. From then on, mentioning this young person's name became our secret weapon to ward off the sadder days with him.

You had to emphasize the J-A-N-E part to get the total result, but his face instantly lit up like a child drawn to cotton candy. As soon as the second part rolled from our lips, K would be silly, filled with silent giggles.

There was just something about hearing it that magically set him into a jovial orbit every time. It was an elixir for the instant formation of a gummy Kaden smile. No matter the circumstance, from needles to the loss of his trademark green pinkie, whatever caused that bottom lip to become apparent could indeed be cured by the utterance of those two words. Watching him laugh when hearing the sound of her name was priceless.

When we find humor in something, it makes sense to continue and enjoy it. You would not believe the total number of times this unique, two-word combination had been uttered in our house through those early years. It made no sense why this name made for such a spirited response; it simply did. Watching his face beam each time was almost indescribable. Since K made little to no sounds orally, his quiet belly laughs showed widely on his face each time.

He was ridiculous with laughter.

We all enjoy seeing or hearing things that make us chuckle whenever we are exposed to them. How many times have you listened to the same comedy routine and still find it as funny now as it was the first time you experienced it?

I know that a few movies will always make me smile at the holidays, though I have watched them each season for years. For Kaden, like repeating the same script, he was never tired or desensitized to hearing those two words. We had our new way of keeping him smiling and grinning most of the time.

To this day, I have no real idea who she is, nor can I answer why or how pronouncing those words gave Kaden such a vital source of humor. There is almost a sort of irony here; it brings new meaning to the phrase "What's in a name?" Go figure.

Maybe I should send her parents a thank-you note for their choice in naming their daughter Olivia Jane. They could never have imagined the impact their decision to name their child Olivia Jane would have on our lives from 2006 to 2009.

I guess you never know.

EIGHTH INNING

* * *

BEYOND

SATURDAY, MAY 3, 2008

Today, it happened again. It was now as if the humming sound was intentionally meant to be heard.

I watched TV downstairs, and Stacey was changing K in his room. The taunting noise started instantly as she stood there with K at the changing table. She called me quickly to validate the event and that she was not going crazy. I waited for the commercial on TV and marched up the stairs, defiantly anticipating to listen to absolutely nothing, yet again.

But, this time, sure as anything, I could finally hear it, too!

The sound was a dull, humming, unwavering, and monotonous tone. The thing was constant and, at the same time, extremely mysterious to try and figure out where it was emanating from.

Now, the once elusive audible drone continued without a break and never waffled by pitch. Today was different; it didn't appear that the sound would stop anymore. Somehow, we had crossed over into a new realm.

"You are right, Stacey; what is that?"

The unwelcome noise was now super noticeable. No effort was needed to listen in around the walls to make it out; it was apparent.

We did have a hard-wired security alarm system throughout the house, so I could quickly rule out any potential battery issues with the units in any of the rooms.

After moving all of the furniture away from the walls and looking for a random toy that might have been causing the strange and annoying buzz, nothing was to be discovered.

Stacey had already done this many times, but we did it together again and then took all the toys out of his room just to be sure.

Every outlet in there—in Aryn's room, the bathroom, the upstairs office, the main bedroom, and the upstairs hallway—was cleared of items plugged in.

Theoretically, no power was drawn up there, yet the sound continued.

Because it wasn't ceasing, we had to take it to a new level of root cause analysis. Thinking perhaps a loose wire or electricity was escaping from the wall, we called a local electrician to examine all of the outlets and test the wiring throughout our entire home.

He remained in our home for approximately two hours, testing and surveying everything that might have been potentially causing this to happen. It was a costly job, but we needed peace of mind that our home wasn't at risk of burning down.

A fire suppression system was installed already, but since this was an electrical phenomenon, the potential for a different mess was of concern. We needed to be thorough by ruling out each cause.

Surprisingly, our first attempt to diagnose the source came without him finding anything wrong, but not before leaving us with a massive bill for his investigative time.

Like us, he had no idea what the cause of it was coming from.

What the heck did it mean, and why?

KANDLE

SUNDAY, MAY 4, 2008

My job continued to afford me tremendous opportunities to partake in many very cool experiences. I had access to places, people, and events most could never imagine. In addition to being a blast to attend, these perks were a nice distraction from the high pressure of day-to-day business operations and also an enjoyable way to invest in my spiritual sanity.

You know you are in a unique space when one weekend finds you on a plane to Key West or in California wine country for four days. On another, you are walking a red carpet at an exclusive gala next to Michael Jordan, Dennis Rodman, Larry Bird, and Magic Johnson. During these years, the fast lane became a blur for me because I never passed up on the chance to live the life of an unknown celebrity.

The circles I traveled in and had access to were nothing short of amazing. Not bad stuff for a troubled kid from humble beginnings who came from a small town by the lakes in New Hampshire. The stories I can tell now would suffice for a lifetime. Once, I even made Jim Carrey laugh so hard he spit out his drink!

I continued to hide my daily anxieties about the Kaden stuff from everyone. During the week, I'd take pictures and sip wine with celebrities, and on weekends, I'd face the tremendous medical unknowns with my family. Talk about an odd juxtaposition.

Keep on smiling, keep on traveling, keep on refilling the glass, and keep on pretending. When you do this, eventually, it catches up with you. (It did for me later on.) Though I constantly spoke to my team about being well-balanced between work and family, my example was hardly influential.

Fast and hard was my way of life now. I was caught up in it all.

Today was the first time we'd enjoyed Kaden's birthday together since birth. A year ago, on his first, unfortunate luck would have it that we were still doing the hospital dance by existing as best we could in two places.

That was all okay; things were different now. We were getting back on track; spring was in full bloom, and our long-lost friend, **Normalcy,** slowly appeared more and more around us.

The day was lovely, aside from him having a second fever in two weeks, seemingly coming out of nowhere. We dismissed it as being just another byproduct of his size and condition.

Two years represented a huge milestone for all of us. It was incredible to think about the long road we had traveled with him, and here we were!

Today was the opportunity to restore the complicated side of our destiny. His birthday was a time to conclude the countless chapters of unforeseen medical ordeals and learnings we had shared over two years with him.

We battled back from the dreadful visit to the doctor in February of 2006 when we were told Stacey would miscarry. After driving home, we sat silently, trying to make sense of the news we had just heard.

We still persevered and never accepted not having any chance.

Weeks later, we listened for hours in a Boston hospital about how our baby could have a quality of life not worth living if he survived birth. We pushed ahead.

We shared disturbing conversations on many different occasions, and while most people would run from them at record speed. We learned to ask questions while seeking more answers.

After rallying hard after being cautioned for such a low success rate for K's delivery, we remained hopeful and looked for a glimmer of *chance*.

We waited, seeking clarity on the condition of our twenty-ounce miracle, wondering if he was alive or dead without any answers immediately forthcoming.

After open-heart surgery, we sat together in the waiting room for our repaired little patient to be wheeled back to his room. Eventually, he awoke to our collective signs of relief many hours later.

We rejoiced on the day Kaden could finally breathe independently. The horrific-looking rubber tube was removed from our baby's throat, only to be replaced by another via a hole cut through his skin into his stomach so he could hold down his feeds. But this was okay, and we believed we were still making progress.

Waiting patiently for the next word to come after Kaden coded several times in his sleep, Stacy and I sat on the edge while racing down to Boston again for more information while they stabilized him.

Glass continuously cracked under our feet as trips to Boston extended into week-long or month-long ordeals more often than not. Yet, for the sake of our son, we begrudgingly broke more and more panes of them as frequently as necessary.

Stacey and I existed with pins and needles repeatedly sticking in us for twenty-four months straight.

And even then, there was more because of the mess we went through before his birth in those earlier months. I could go on and on; these were just some of the talking points. What an incredible run we had with this child.

None of this had beaten us.

Hope and **Circumstance** asked us to trust them early on, and we did so without blinking or flinching. In doing so, Stacey and I became stronger.

This was all a part of the Kaden deal.

Finally, and deservingly, on his second birthday, it was time for us to become a family. We'd taken enough wild rides over the last seven years. Our opportunity to get off the coaster and onto the merry-go-round was upon us.

On May 5, 2008, we stood on the threshold of becoming typical for the first time. Our unwanted thirst for adversity had finally and mercifully been quenched.

Happy Birthday.

What a present.

BAFFLE

SATURDAY, MAY 17, 2008

When a creepy noise continuously makes itself known upstairs, you can't just pretend and hope for it to disappear. By now, the bizarre sound was incessant from morning until night and even while we all slept. Amazingly, Kaden didn't seem deprived by it. Our little guy dreamed right through it.

Today, we called another general contractor to test his expertise and see if he might have any luck. It might have been ours if the low droning, continuous sound stopped before he got there to troubleshoot and investigate. This certainly would have made the two of us look downright foolish. The odds were low if this was the case by now. The sound wasn't going away.

We already knew how his inspection would end, but what the heck?

Arriving confidently and stepping with the swagger of a well-seasoned craftsman, he entered our home and marched from room to room. He was hearing the curious sound in its full glory. It soon became apparent that he was increasingly puzzled, like all of us.

This failed visitor was not forty-five minutes into his time with us. After a shoulder shrug and a half-smile, off he went.

If nothing else, we had peace of mind between those first two guys; there was no imminent fire danger in the walls. Their time wasn't a total waste for us.

We may have placed a turnstile at the entrance and charged folks to come and experience this strange phenomenon for themselves. To this day, I can still recall the sound; it was borderline ominous.

They say persistence always pays off. Next in line that Sunday were two local civil workers from Peterborough to diagnose the mysterious Morrison moaning room!

I believe it might have been the chief, but whoever from the fire department arrived confidently and marched up the stairs directly into K's room to listen for himself. He was our next challenger to enter into this Morrison family mystery episode.

I'm sure he was less than pleased to leave the station on his way home to come and diagnose our auditory mess. It would have been more acceptable all the way around if he had known upfront that he was about to be schooled quickly by our curious phenomenon!

We laughed before his arrival, knowing his trip here to see and hear this odd sound would end like every other visitor had, without any answers.

Finding nothing at all, he made small talk with us after about an hour before conceding that he had never experienced anything like it in all his years on the force.

Our calling him and then the local police department were our two last-ditch efforts to find the cause and solution to our odd dilemma.

Per our request, the Peterborough officer pulled up in an official capacity to investigate next. After arriving and parking his cruiser, Aryn watched him walk up the granite steps and knock on our front door.

By now, you can guess where this one was headed!

Upon crossing the threshold, we all silenced immediately as he heard the strange sound for the first time. It was as apparent as the wind blowing in your face, with incredible clarity, easily audible the entire time.

"What the hell is that?" he remarked quizzically as he made his way up the stairs to Kaden's bedroom.

Quite obviously puzzled, he inspected, re-inspected, and checked some more as every other person had done before him.

We watched this poor fellow examine the outlets, go to the attic section above the bedroom, and then survey the entire upstairs living area for anything appearing to be afoul with wiring or some other trigger that could be causing this constant monotone sound to drone on constantly.

He was astonished at the seeming lack of source and found nothing out of place; the same reaction as the other three.

The poor guy joked to us while standing there, shaking his head back and forth, chuckling, "This is my first haunted experience."

Jokingly, he was also perplexed about how to write the report to document this investigation without sounding like he was entirely out of his tree!

While it might have been great to discover the cause, at least we would have it officially on record now by the fire and the police departments. How interesting to go back someday and read the reports and see how each of wrote this up from their perspectives.

In summary, four professionals witnessed our perplexing fun precisely as it happened in real time. Aside from having documentation to validate our story, we never got any real answers from them.

At this point, I don't attribute what happened in our home to anything other than the supernatural. There is absolutely zero reason for this to happen, as it did in our house that spring. Fifteen years later, my belief still stands.

This was otherworldly.

"The White Lady" was back, trying to get our attention.

YANKEE

MONDAY, MAY 19, 2008

The temperature had dropped significantly since earlier, when I grabbed my jacket and hurried to my car to meet my friend Mark at the hotel. He was born and raised in New Jersey and has always made what I would consider poor choices for sports fandom. It wasn't his fault; clearly, he was misled into following the wrong teams from an early age.

Nevertheless, tonight was the annual event whereby I would allow a dreaded Yankee fan to accompany me through the hallowed gates of Fenway Park to witness the World Champion Boston Red Sox do what they do best for the next several hours.

I expected him to be on his very best behavior, as I would not think twice about taking this privilege away from him and awarding the honor to another friend. This was an opportunity, not a guarantee! One wisecrack out of his mouth about the team or the fans, and quicker than you can say, "We're off to see the wizard," I would see to it that he was quickly off on his way down Boylston trying to make friends with the sausage and onion guys.

Damn Yankee fan.

The Red Sox were the hottest ticket in town in 2008, as I would have been remiss if I had failed to make this quite clear to Mark on numerous occasions in the days leading up to the game. This endeavor was not easy, as I justified my bringing him as somehow being for the sport's good.

Perhaps I had temporarily taken leave of my senses as if I were now some sports diplomat tasked with bringing unity amongst various fan bases. In this instance, my challenge would be getting common respect between the Sox and Yankee fans.

If you grow up in New England, you know about shoveling snow, love lobster, miss one letter from your alphabet (R), and dislike all New York sports teams. Here I was, getting ready to enjoy America's favorite pastime with him.

Go figure.

Last year, Yankee Fan and I walked to the field before the game to check things out. After we got there, he quickly called his son to tell him he was at Fenway Park for the first time and touching the ballpark soil. For all the crap I gave him for being a fan of the other team, it was fantastic to be a part of this baseball memory of his.

Ironically, he was about to be a part of mine that night.

Mark is a good friend who could genuinely appreciate this ballpark's history, sport, and spectacle. Because of his love for baseball, it was nice to be able to make this happen for him, too. Our time together at any sporting event has always been fun, as our passion for various sports is not limited to baseball. Being a Patriots fan and him being a Jets fan also provided us the opportunity for some good-spirited banter during football season.

I had looked forward to this night for many personal reasons, plus the opportunity to remind him frequently that the Sox are the World Champions and the Yankees are not.

As we enjoyed a couple of Fenway franks and a few ice-cold beers, the joy of being there on this night in May was ever-present. I recall sitting in the concourse before the game, absolutely loving where my life was finally headed. A handful of days prior was Kaden's birthday, and positive momentum was building.

The ballgame progressed slowly, as the opposing team had no offense. There were no hits!

John Lester had been pitching a masterful game, marching the Sox into the middle of the seventh inning with a hitless and score-less performance thus far. As the familiar chorus of "Sweet Caro-line" played loudly, the traditional seven-thinning Fenway sing-a-long with 37,000 of my closest friends had begun.

We sang like old drunks getting together again in a rundown Irish Tavern. At least for the song's sake, we all become unified in purpose for about three minutes.

When we finished attempting to shout out the lyrics off-key, the Yankee Fan next dared to ask me if we did this at every home game. I shook my head in disgust and remarked, "Of course," as if this were not anything but common knowledge.

After this remark, he might have been asked to leave had he been naive to Fenway Franks. Luckily for him, this knowledge single-handedly kept him in the ballpark. But man, he came close to having to watch the remainder of the game from a local bar!

You can remove the fans from New York but never rely on them to have the wisdom to become part of Sox Nation.

Damn Yankee fan.

As has been my protocol for some time now, I prepared Mark earlier that day to beat the traffic out of Fenway Park; we would need to leave shortly after that seventh-inning stretch and finish the game at the hotel bar.

The last time I had done this, David Ortiz hit a walk-off home run in the bottom of the ninth to clinch the victory for the Sox. Sometimes, it pays not to leave early!

On this evening, thankfully, we decided not to.

Jon Lester pitched his first complete game in the major leagues that night. This alone made for a special one, but there was more to this story. An exclamation point was appropriate for this occurrence.

History was made uniquely, too, after he recorded the last of three outs against the Kansas City Royals in the top of the ninth in no-hitter fashion!

How appropriate, I thought. Here I was, sitting at what was potentially my first and last no-hitter I would ever have seen—at that instant.

What were the odds?

The game was notable, Kaden was doing well, and my life was finally headed precisely where it was supposed to go. The night was the epitome of calm as I finally settled down and decompressed.

It all happened with perfect timing.

Aside from the no-hitter, what was more compelling to me was how Lester had dealt with a medical ordeal in his recent past. He had been battling cancer two years before and was in remission. His fight was highly publicized locally; we all knew about it.

The visual of the then-Red Sox skipper Terry Francona embracing this courageous survivor at the end of the game brought tears to my eyes. The game was one for the ages. How fortunate I was to have been there with Yankee Fan.

Life was good.

"So good, so good, so good."

TRIPLE

My employment was secure in those most uncertain times. I enjoyed my work and the people I did it with. The company was progressive, so there were always many exciting things happening. My sense of accomplishment became real for a guy who spent his entire life with low self-esteem.

Our corporate stock had been consistently rising, so financial struggles were few and far between. We were comfortable in our current economic situation, from stock options to restricted stock grants to making bonuses each year; we even discussed loosely purchasing a new and bigger home.

Thankfully, our fear of Aryn needing corrective surgery for his head was also becoming increasingly distant in the rearview mirror of life. The fluid was draining on its own slowly as he also grew more and more into his head size with each birthday. There was much more going on with him at the time, but we didn't know until many years later. He had many other psychological and mental health concerns, but the Hydrocephalus he faced no longer appeared to be of much trouble.

It was becoming a distant worry from two overly cautious newlyweds and fizzling out almost a decade later. We were blessed to have dodged that bullet. There was damage, but not in the physical sense.

Last night, I sat at a Red Sox game, genuinely feeling blessed to be there in full enjoyment without some of the previous stressors blocking my happiness. It symbolically also underscored our positive shift.

At breakfast today, Yankee Fan and I joked about how much fun we'd had and marveled again that we were fortunate to watch history unfold. Almost as though it was meant to be. We just happened to be at the right game on the right night of the week and in the right month for baseball. Since the Sox play 162 games annually, you can determine our odds of being there for this one.

That ballpark is magic, I tell you—pure magic.

A week before last night's event, my music obsession was blessed by my ability to attend a concert I had wanted to have happen for almost twenty years. The opportunity to see one of my favorite bands, The Cure, at a local venue very quickly placed me enthusiastically as high as the sky while watching from my front-row seat.

This band had influenced me for decades, and finally, seeing them live was just about the greatest gift ever for a guy who lives and breathes tonality and lyrics. It was truly the culmination of a bucket list item. Music is so important to me that most will never understand. My being there was selfishly cathartic.

To see them on stage in front of me playing those critical songs was far beyond my expectations. I was blown away by the sound and visual representation that complemented each note flawlessly. My inner joy during that show was unmatched.

I leaned on many of their songs during my more challenging early days after Dad passed away. This music catalog helped me get through them and beyond. Previously several years earlier, there was a chance to see them in Jersey, where I was working, but it never panned out. Boston was my hometown, so for me, it was much more special to experience them there for the first time.

My kid brother, Brendan, canceled at the last minute, so I went alone. It made absolutely no difference at all. Everything on this night was done with peace of mind—the ability to soak in the music as it absorbed into my skin during every song.

The event was absolute heaven. This is as close as I could have come if one could genuinely walk on air.

If things had been different with Kaden, I might not have had the opportunity to see the concert or that ballgame. Both were still throwing fantastic imagery impressions my way. My internal permagrin did all the talking for me on these two subjects.

In ten more days, unbelievably, I was booked on a promotional opportunity to play golf with New England sports figure Tom Brady on an all expenses-paid trip to Santa Monica. Yes, I would swing a golf club and have some one-on-one time with TB-12 for one hole of golf.

Talk about three reasons to smile emphatically. Figuratively, I'd hit the lottery.

According to Stacey, the mysterious noise in Kaden's room had suddenly stopped this morning. (You can't make this stuff up.)

Did I mention yet that life was really, really good?

NINETH INNING

* * *

HAIR

TUESDAY, MAY 20,2008

W hat struck me most about this time was how we were about to become quite comfortable together as the family I had always imagined having. Oddly, it took us nine years into our marriage to believe this. I know I did.

Now was an opportunity to slow again for the first time in what seemed to be forever.

Sure, with Kaden, there would always be some medical turmoil, but generally speaking, our lives calmed down. We realized some positive momentum, and it was just fantastic. It was the first time I had been afforded to feel this way in years—not having many worries at all other than the mundane, our turn to relax—the perfect storm of positivity we had been hoping for.

Living close to friends and family again allowed us to attend birthday and holiday events and do things that large families enjoy doing.

When you suffer from manic depression and anxiety, there is always a constant imbalance. When the days are bad, they compound; when good, they ease the emotional state only slightly. In my case, for the only time as far back as I can recall, that spring, I honestly was in a great place. The weight they once had on me seemed to be subsiding, finally allowing me to breathe in the air of positivity again. The purest I could have inhaled. It was the first deep, cleansing breath I was fortunate to consume in a long, long while, believing our lives had finally started to align.

As written earlier, Jeff played a unique role in this story. He has for most of my life. The guy with the bowel issue and too much body hair, who lives in the basement of his parent's home, sets sail on a cruise ship by himself, leaves messages repeatedly at 3 a.m., and genuinely cares about my family, has been next to me through thick and thin.

It may seem obvious here, but as days shine bright, we want to share them with people who can understand and appreciate our happiness. Nothing is better than a celebration with good friends and family at those milestones in our lives. Think back about some of yours; I guarantee those folks have walked a thousand miles with you.

Admirably, when days are not so good, the people on the other end of the phone will always listen without hesitation or judgment. They are always the first folks to immediately offer moral support and help in whatever way is appropriate for the circumstance.

My afternoon proceeded as usual, with my catching up on phone messages. I owed Jeff a return call and saw no better opportunity to rub in my attendance at the ballgame that previous evening.

I figured, once again, that a call with him would provide me with the perfect opportunity to recount my recent good fortunes regarding The Cure concert and the Sox game and to mention once again that I was going to be playing golf with the Super Bowl MVP Tom Brady the following week.

During previous conversations regarding Kaden and Aryn, Jeff always responded with well-thought-out questions based on his information. He then always provided his perception of the situation. Whether or not I agreed with his assessments didn't matter. I appreciated his offering up some new ways of looking at things. He isn't a deep thinker, but Jeffrey is very detail-oriented regarding sharing.

Thoughtfully, he asks about K in every phone conversation I have had with him since his birth, hanging on to every word. He always takes the time to remember dates, milestones, and critical moments in our children's lives. These are more routine check-in calls where we share much information within a wide range of topics.

Today's conversation began in the usual manner, with small talk regarding his recent vacation, the stock market, oil prices, and then onto the welfare of Kaden. It was a typical call filled with lots of agenda items.

We began by highlighting a few details of the Sox game, comparing notes about what the team did right and where they may have made a few errors. As usual, he did most of the talking for this one. It is interesting to hear his perspective on baseball.

Most don't know; I played on his team when we were young. He often pulled the grass out in centerfield while looking the other way during our games. There may have been a focus issue or two within him. Let's agree that, as a position player, he may not have been one of our core strengths.

We then reviewed the latest Kaden information that Tuesday. There was some insight into previous medical ailments we had gone through with our son and not chosen to share with anyone up to that point.

There we were, on the phone, laughing once again about the past, catching up on the latest music news, and reviewing various stock performances. It was a light-hearted and oddly refreshing opportunity to converse about nothing.

While talking, I watched an individual sit in the car next to me at the Milford, NH, Irving station with the windows rolled up, holding a cigarette in his hand. This is a common sight, but something about this struck me odd while listening to Jeff.

This smoker was next to me for a reason.

Of all the places to be parked, I was beside a person with a curious perspective on taking things for granted. My little boy had stopped breathing again during one of his most recent hospital stays; his lungs desperately tried to work as designed. If only they could do so consistently. And here I sat in my car next to this dude who was puffing away frantically as though those lit sticks were some new drug.

With each one, an inhale of toxic chemicals followed by exhaling white smoke. Over and over again, he dragged on the remains of the cigarette without care as to what it may be doing to him in the long run. Here he was, given the gift of healthy lungs with the ability to breathe all the glorious fresh air he could with them but consciously elected not to.

What an odd juxtaposition.

The second part of our touch-base call finished with Jeff requesting updates regarding Kaden and Aryn's health. He knew in detail most of our journeys with both boys and was always one person I felt I could confide in with some personal reflections without any judgment.

As Jeffrey and I sufficiently reviewed all topics on our lists, we ended the conversation an hour and a half later with one more interesting tidbit. While it seemed inconsequential then, it all changed in less than a day.

When changing Kaden the previous morning, I was perplexed to discover that his g-tube was wholly pushed out from his belly. The damn thing popped out entirely; it isn't designed to happen so easily without forcing it. For this anomaly to occur on its own requires a lot of finagling; Kaden wouldn't do it to himself with his hands.

The entire apparatus had to have been pushed out from the inside. It left the gaping, exposed hole in his gut that I saw when changing him.

Why did this happen?

I shared the story, and we quickly surmised it wasn't any big deal. To be truthful, the sight of an exposed hole in his stomach with fluid oozing out was still more of a concern at the moment than the reason why it had come out.

His belly felt stiff, like he was slightly bloated, but neither Stacey nor I thought anything more. After a bit of finagling with syringes and careful reinsertion, it went back.

The afternoon ended as well as it might have, with two friends sharing one more laugh and a few more minutes of silliness. It is a wonder how much time we waste sending text messages to one another!

Another story for another day.

The last thing I had said to him concerning Kaden was, "We were kidding ourselves to think that we would have a child born under such dire circumstances without having to endure some challenges along the way."

Ironically, I made this statement less than twenty-four hours before a series of occurrences were set in motion, ultimately changing our lives forever.

NO

WEDNESDAY, MAY 21, 2008

I love the spring season, even more so as I have aged. There is a carefree and easy spirit all about this time of year. Where I live in the northeast, the grass begins to wake, the wind blows a little warmer, and the opportunity for new growth is apparent.

As we headed toward Memorial Day Weekend, a sense of loose excitement ran through our house regarding plans for extended family fun at the ocean on this awakening start to the day. I recall it well because the sun was shining early, and the potential to get things done professionally was my mission on this one because of it.

Before heading out, I walked to the kitchen, greeted Aryn and Kaden, made two slices of toast, poured coffee, and reviewed my schedule with Stacey for the week. I did it without much thought; we were sitting in any kitchen in any town in America—another day to begin like so many others.

She had taken Kaden back to Children's Hospital at Dartmouth (CHAD) the previous week for painful abdominal issues, but nothing about his condition was of any obvious conversation. We could tell he was in discomfort, trying to make whatever bothered him disappear. Because he was nonverbal, it was challenging to understand his pain level or other medical complexities. Over time, you tend to be able to read minor signs and interpret them.

Today was one of those days.

I remarked to her before I left that he appeared "off," as Kaden was sitting in his bouncy seat rather lifelessly in between having fits due to something bothering him. He still had a pattern of being a passive baby, but this level of lethargy was noticeably next level, even for him.

His mannerisms didn't seem significant enough to draw further attention to it other than my quick mention. Since he was under-going so much medical stuff, he had every right to be mellow and take things in stride. Maybe it was just one of those days when the entire body didn't feel like doing much. Who knew?

I never thought twice about it at any other point after dropping Aryn off at school and heading down to Cape Cod for work. Listening to sports radio, I reclined slightly and cruised south at an average speed.

Confirming our plans to get away and shine some positive light in my direction, I phoned home on the way down to suggest we use our summer cottage in Maine for the long holiday weekend. Because we reside in a tiny community where woods surrounded our home, time at the ocean was a form of most welcome escapism.

Unfortunately, we had not been able to use it that much in the previous twelve months since the purchase. We intended to spend as much summer there as possible moving forward. Due to Kaden's constant medical imbalance and frequent visits to the hospital, it simply hadn't worked out as planned. But that was okay. This summer, we hoped to make up for all those lost days.

Our place there has a large deck to the front built perfectly for quiet time and contemplation. In the morning, while enjoying a cup of warmth, the smell of freshly baked doughnuts from the business up the road frequently enhances the experience of watching the sun rise over the horizon and reflect off the water.

Sitting outside with a glass in hand can only be described as a source of complete and total peace on warm summer evenings when the wind blows, spreading calm throughout.

My anxiety was super high this week, knowing I had two full days of touring people around an area that was utterly unfamiliar to me. These market rides always caused stress, so mine was already in rare form as early as ten that morning.

Looking forward to the simple upcoming pleasures of spending the holiday weekend with my family motivated me to get through that week and enjoy those planned days again.

The intense schedule had me spend the first evening in Plymouth, MA, and then picking up the executives at the airport in Hyannis that morning. We were scheduled to spend the day together, have a fine dinner, and finish the drive the next morning on Friday. It was a lot of riding while looking at real estate, but not too bad compared to other tours I'd done. Still, it carried a lot of nerves to do and say the right things.

Thus far, after arriving, my entire time was spent gathering information on a potential real estate acquisition while mapping out the route to find each location, hoping to minimize the traffic along the way. One wrong turn, and I would have looked like a numbskull getting us lost! The corporate plane was coming; the timing was super important.

I recall thinking it odd as my phone vibrated while looking down and seeing a call from Stacey coming in since we had already talked earlier. This series of calls and the other one during 9/11 resonate with me deeply still.

In general, having a child born at twenty ounces, calls of this nature are not necessarily atypical. Most didn't create a sense of drama or panic within me after having fielded countless others during the last two years with Kaden and early on with Aryn.

With Stacey's crude diagnosis of his stomach looking larger and him acting constantly fussy, I saw no reason to conclude that anything significant was happening with our youngest son after hearing her version of what was taking place back home. (Then again, I cannot swing a hammer or make a pizza; what did I know about these matters?)

We decided she would keep a watchful eye on him and get through the day. My mind was so distracted with work that I was almost dismissive of hearing any of this. There was too much other business going on that day.

Upon hanging up, I did feel concerned as a parent to know that my child was in pain, but I fully expected to find out later that Kaden was just gassy or that one of his many medications was not reacting well with him. Because of my preoccupation with the tour, it quickly rolled away from me.

We were already on a wait-and-see timing schedule from the most recent series of tests, but something inside Stacey was nagging at her.

They say only a mother can tell, right?

Stacey continued seeking answers and getting more information about his obvious pain and what could be causing the port around his g-tube to push it out. What exactly was suddenly causing his belly size to increase and his general condition to be so poor?

After about an hour after calling me, the two of them went to see his local pediatrician, "Dr. C," for passive reassurance and peace of mind since he knew our son so well.

Because of his familiarity with Kaden, it made sense to have his pediatric doctor check out Kaden that afternoon and get his thoughts on what he felt might be happening. (What a credit to the persistence of a mother to know when something is wrong with her child and not settle on a dismissive diagnosis.) At the very least, he might provide some assurance that there was nothing significant for us to be concerned about.

Stacey called me again that afternoon, marking our third phone conversation since I'd left our house.

Seeing the phone vibrating yet again on my front seat angered me. Before answering, I assumed it was another follow-up to our Maine conversation since I didn't know she had taken K to see his doctor.

Perhaps this time was as simple as her wanting to finalize whether we were grilling dogs, burgers, or steaks at the cottage. I didn't have much patience for this nonsense either way; my guests were arriving in the morning! I was too busy and focused to be distracted.

I quickly learned that the doctor ordered Kaden to be immediately transported to Dartmouth Hitchcock Medical Center in Lebanon, NH, as fast as my wife could drive them there.

CRASH

The damn pins and needles up and down my spine immediately returned as I sat in the front seat of the rented SUV in Hyannis. The thoughts of a car accident or tragedy in the family always tend to be my first assumption at times like this. When your wife calls you in such an affected state, one cannot help but immediately assume the worst.

It took a while for Stacey's voice to calm down. She rambled on, trying to get her words out and pleading with me for help.

She was fast approaching an entirely new traumatic place. One I never knew existed within her after all those years. This put things into perspective about where we were, in crisis without answers.

Frantic, panic-stricken, and unable to speak in clear sentences now, the only part I could gather initially was that something pretty scary must have been going on with Kaden or had already happened to him.

We knew this would be a long road with him; was it all starting up again?

I had shared a lot of details with my boss, William, regarding my son being born prematurely two years ago, and he knew how delicate parenthood was for us even still. There was always something going on for me to share when we got together.

I called back to the office to let him know I could not pick him or the others up from the corporate jet in the morning. While speaking, it was apparent my mind was all over the place as those sentences were short and not framed well in a cut-and-paste sort of way.

Without hesitation, he offered to have the company arrange and pay for a car service to drive me from Cape Cod to Hanover, NH, immediately, no questions asked.

He was prepared to get things in motion and make them happen for me, at the very least, to take away the burden of the two-hundred-mile drive in traffic to rush up to the hospital.

There was concern about my ability to drive safely under the circumstances; while the gesture was highly kind, I had no minutes to wait for this to be arranged.

Feeling like time would not favor me, I declined and hauled ass toward NH.

The drive from Cape Cod to Dartmouth Hitchcock Medical Center is daunting, even more so heading into a popular travel weekend. This sheer amount of traffic on the roads created much frustration and perhaps a bit too much extra time to speculate on the condition and diagnosis of my baby. Thankfully, I was heading off it, as most travelers were heading in the opposite direction.

Looking at the road ahead and utterly unaware of what was happening around me, my immediate thoughts were also for my wife. I could not even imagine what she must have felt while rushing to get him to the hospital on that ninety-minute trip up north from the doctor's office in Peterborough.

The feeling of helplessness while sitting behind the wheel weighed enormously. A part of me attempted to remain the ever-present stoic individual I had always been while dealing with these medical uncertainties concerning Kaden. This new situation made it more challenging due to the quick timing of it and my unanswered questions surrounding his current condition.

There was a fight to maintain the balance between justification and rational thinking. While driving eighty miles an hour to get back up there, I was one part hesitant; the other part of me remained a realist. Kaden wasn't born perfect; his body was far from it.

Was this another part of our unique story with him?

Because this mess had evolved rapidly, there wasn't much time to obsess about causal possibilities. How the emotions might sort out wouldn't be known until I arrived at Dartmouth Hitchcock several hours later.

Several times in the following phone conversation, I asked Stacey to calm down and slowly tell me all the details.

Several of Kaden's organs were beginning to shut down simultaneously for some unknown reason.

The images taken earlier of his abdomen confirmed Kaden's liver and spleen were also severely distended. He had a high fever, was in extreme pain, and now was drifting in and out of consciousness.

If this wasn't enough to hear from hours away by car, another sentence began to roll off her lips.

There was more for me to know.

Unbelievably, while crying hysterically, the last words I could make out before we hung up was that Kaden's tiny heart was failing and could stop beating at any time.

Stacey hysterically shouted on the phone for me to get to the hospital, "NOW!"

I feared my child would die before I made it up to Hanover.

WHO

Dartmouth Hitchcock is a top care facility. Growing up in NH, you appreciate its importance in treating people with severe illnesses. I had always known of this place as one where you never wanted to find yourself because your presence would indicate severe illness. If you do, take solace in this facility's caring team of professionals.

They are awesome.

Stacey's stepfather, George, received a kidney transplant there a few years back, so we were exposed to their talents firsthand. They would surely be able to provide timely answers and a diagnosis.

For what it was worth, amidst the day's confusion, it relieved me to know my child was on his way to such a well-respected establishment for care. At least we had that going for us.

If his heart was going, it was only a matter of time before it stopped beating. There are no words to write here that can accurately describe this horror.

Stacey might be all alone with Kaden when he took his final breath.

There is no fairness in trauma; I now understand this.

I was helpless to do anything but drive as fast as I could and pray for the next four hours. Funny, I am the least religious person I know, and there I was, begging for help.

After what I can only sum up as one of the most stressful trips of my life, I finally arrived with the nerves of a man on stage in front of a thousand people for the first time. It was the single most horrific event to have ever happened to me to that point.

This one torments me even still.

Finding a parking spot was not an issue; it seemed to be of minimal reward. Due to the uncertainty, I jogged from my car to the building without spending time walking.

How was our son? What was I about to encounter? Stacey and I hadn't spoken for a while, so everything was a mystery. The information desk saw I was distraught and walked with me up to our patient room.

Kaden was in a full-sized bed. Seeing him on a big boy mattress and box spring was odd. For starters, he always slept in a crib at home, so the site of his tiny body in this one seemed instantly off.

He was connected to several IVs and other large machinery staged around his bed. Once again, all sorts of gruesome tubes and wires were intertwined uncomfortably around his body as well. This throwback look was a reminder of his birth some two years prior, only now he was larger and in critical condition for another reason.

Generally, for a parent, the visual of seeing one's child hooked up to so much medical equipment can create a tremendous sense of uneasiness. Even if the circumstances are not that critical regarding medical urgency, the noises, machines, tubes, and lines add a certain level of drama. For us, towers and all that other monitoring busyness were nothing new.

Our two-year-old's impending heart failure urgency was.

Ironically, this time too, it wasn't the equipment freaking me out and causing anxiety but the actual sight of my son. He was weak, glossy-eyed, and barely recognizable. Kaden looked like he belonged to someone else.

His skin color was off, almost a pasty, pale white. Was this my son, or had someone been trying to play a cruel joke by switching him with someone else's sickly toddler? If this was my boy who lay before me, he was in terrible shape.

Seeing our sick toddler in his hospital bed was rough; he was in so much pain and heartbreakingly terrible shape. I had seriously underestimated the apparent discomfort of our baby until now.

This child was noticeably bloated around his belly, constantly moving from side to side, trying to find comfort. Seeing him do this over and over again was heartbreaking. He didn't understand why he felt this way and repeatedly searched for a comfortable solution to his pain. For a child who made no sound, you could see he was in tremendous discomfort by his constant wincing.

I was surprised they hadn't yet given him something to either knock him out or minimize his pain. There could be an entirely different protocol when heart function is in question. Without having any information, there wasn't much complaining coming from our end—only trust in these excellent doctors and medical assistants.

His eyes, which had always displayed a certain optimism and innocence, were now two dark marbles staring at everyone he met. He instantly questioned why no one was doing anything to help him feel better.

They, too, were shrieking out with urgency for us all to diagnose his condition. Looking up at me for answers, he resembled an old, frail man moments before closing his tired eyes for good.

My son, who typically was such a fighter, was hardly formidable tonight. He was a beaten shell of himself. In another way, our child reminded me of a certain possessed little girl in a movie from the seventies via his unpredictable flailing around. While driving there, my deductions ranged from heart failure to an infection. There was no preparation for *this* visual reality, regardless of what would ultimately be determined. His condition was much more complicated.

We sat for several hours more without answers, helpless to do anything but sympathize with our writhing child.

Earlier, I'd booked a room at a local hotel for our convenience without thinking Stacey would join me. I knew I would sleep there, though. It made sense instead of driving back to Peterborough to sleep and then turning around and driving all the way back in the morning.

The hotel was only about a mile from the hospital, so Stacey could quickly contact me from Kaden's room in case of any news or sudden trauma. I could get back there at a moment's notice.

Aryn slept in his home bed, dreaming of whatever kids his age dreamt of. He remained at peace for the night, unaware of the massive storm cloud about to settle above his entire family. My mother was at the house again for the night with him, as she had been so many other times to help us out.

Stacey watched TV on an uncomfortable hospital bed beside our sick little boy again. She, too, was unaware of the impending cloud cover moving in overhead.

With a glass of Chardonnay to keep me company at the tiny hotel bar, I sat alone, playing music through my headphones to provide an appropriate soundscape while sifting through my past again, hoping to block out the current chaos.

I felt sick inside; taking over my body was a hectic, racing heart due to these new uncertainties surrounding Kaden's condition. There was only confusion for pondering now, nothing else.

I popped two Ambiens for good measure to help blur the confusion of the day away. They had become a crutch to help me by now. Rarely was it that I traveled without my prescription. So much had gone on over time; sleep was the new enemy. Too many painful shadows lurked in the early morning hours.

Until the pills reacted in my brain, another sip before a new set of question marks raced through my stuffed mind.

Everything was suddenly upside down again.

EXTRA INNING

* * *

SOAK

THURSDAY, MAY 22, 2008

Today began quite similarly for us in a way the previous one had ended. We were without any new answers, our child was still in incredible discomfort, and there seemed to be no additional information coming our way. Lots of tests were being done, but nothing conclusive had surfaced.

These two days were different from the others in our past because of the critical nature of what had been causing such trauma to Kaden. Unfortunately, when you have no answers to medical questions, even the most flavorful cup of java won't take the edge off, no matter how much you consume.

After arriving back at the hospital fairly early, I wasn't prepared to see what I saw this morning: the worst Kaden had ever appeared. You could not mistake his disfigurement by now. His stomach looked like someone had shoved a basketball inside it. His belly was massive.

If yesterday was bad, today was ten times worse. I realized this was undoubtedly becoming more complex than we had initially bargained for.

We were dealing with next-level stuff.

Remarkably, his tummy had now distended to the point that all the veins across it were extremely prominent under the surface of his skin. So much so that you could trace them with your finger; they appeared to stretch as elastic bands do to their thinnest form just before snapping into small pieces. Because his frame was so tiny, it also exaggerated how huge he had become overnight. Seeing this happening to a two-year-old's body was a cause for alarm and an immediate action plan. There was none yet.

His stomach looked like it was on loan from a grown man with a beer gut. The pressure this girth was causing on his entire midsection was indescribable as poor Kaden was continuously writhing around us in his tiny crib, trying to find some way to relieve his back, spine, and torso from the monstrosity that was once his tiny, little belly.

Propped up in bed watching videos, his huge lower region was almost blocking him from seeing the screen. The only minor comfort that eased him slightly was to have his favorite green binkie firmly in his mouth for constant, rapid sucking action. It was of little help when your stomach appeared to be gaining size by the day, but at least it was something.

While holding his hand, his pleading eyes were seeking something neither of us could give him. Aside from medication and sedation, there was nothing we could do to help until we had answers to what was happening and a solution to remedy it. In such a plight, you almost feel like an intentionally neglectful parent. The instincts to aid your child cannot be overstated at such an unsettling time. We were helpless to do anything.

Did any of this have something to do with his deformed stomach and esophagus?

Since we hadn't rescheduled the operation to correct it, was this now somehow the result of it worsening?

Stacey and I worked shifts attending to Kaden while the morning dragged on without a word regarding his situation. We were always in the room and available to meet with the doctors if there was any immediate news.

You can't spend every moment around sick children without becoming personally affected. It is essential to clear your head now and then and break the question mark trance. We routinely took turns going to the café for drinks and snacks and to grab some fresh moments alone to gather our thoughts.

At approximately 2 p.m. that afternoon, a small trickle of information finally came, but it wasn't the comprehensive set of details and facts we'd hoped for. Most of it consisted of conclusions we had already drawn.

They confirmed up to that point that his heart, liver, spleen, and gallbladder were severely enlarged, but the tests were still inconclusive regarding what was causing this. Dumbfounded and partly frustrated, I was unsure how to interpret this basic general update. It seemed to me that any individual of average intelligence could have concluded that a portion of his insides was enlarged. We needed to know WHY!

So, were we any more informed than before?

Were they keeping something from us?

Still, outwardly, they had no potential thoughts on his condition to share. We could sense by how they spoke to us that Kaden's condition was of grave concern to them as much as it was to us. He was being cared for well and taken seriously, for sure.

Again, always searching for the positive: at least his heart had been ruled out for being at risk of immediate failure. That much they were content with sharing. Nothing else came our way, but this was a relief and a start for information to return.

The tests continued. And so, we waited on edge for more news.

To make matters worse, a steady flow was now leaking from inside his midsection through his bowels into his diaper. We found ourselves rapidly changing his clothes and bedding in succession out of necessity as his condition seemed to be rapidly devolving into another phase of criticality.

By nightfall, so much escaped from Kaden that bright rivers soiled everything beneath and around him by the hour.

He was now being routinely colored from head to toe by his own fresh, red blood.

CEILING

T here was no choice in the matter. Our priorities were immediately apparent after now seeing Kaden bleeding from the inside out.

The hotel room was paid for one more evening. It also meant being away from Aryn, which tore at me to leave him home again without either parent for another night with one of his grand-mothers. We did what we felt was right and remained close to Kaden.

Staying by him for the next couple of hours into the evening, we snuck away together once for a few minutes and gathered our thoughts outside his hospital room as he finally drifted off. I am unsure if either knew how to proceed emotionally.

Shit had gone down so fast there hadn't been time to consider our feelings in any substantive way. We had been running and gunning from one conversation to the next; there was no time to decompress until now. It did not appear we would receive any news regarding his diagnosis as the day finally wound down.

Stacey chose to sleep in the hospital room with Kaden and remain by his side. With so much uncertainty ahead, I wanted to ensure we had a place to sleep and escape from that medical environment as needed. The hotel was there again for me.

Though slumbering in the hospital next to your child is an option, the reality in my mind was that it was less than optimal for two parents who need to remain grounded to be crammed together on a tiny cot. To do so, you must be willing to submit nightly to an alien onslaught of sounds associated with such a stay. To me, it just didn't seem prudent.

I drove back to the Courtyard late and conversed briefly with the young women at the front desk. The entire conversational exchange was brief yet on point.

I told her my two-year-old child was admitted after being frantically rushed there a day earlier. She looked at my unsettled eyes and wished me well for the following day.

She, in return, told me that she had lost her then-two-year-old brother. She also appeared sympathetic to our child, being only two and in the hospital, as her brother was. I could tell she was still in a very profoundly saddened place just by how she looked at me while sharing her story. I could also tell she wanted to offer more but was holding back.

When you are dealing with your urgencies, it is heavy to hear the plight of other children in addition to your own. It hit home with me a little too much as I offered her my thoughts and listened a bit longer before she asked me to stop by the front desk the next day to let her know what they found out about Kaden. I think she sincerely wanted to be kept updated. My situation was uniquely relatable to her.

As we move about our day often in haste, you never know that chance conversations with strangers can have such a profound impact. Her words rang through my head as I walked away down the hall toward the corridor on the right.

This poor soul was hurting and wanted to keep her brother's memory alive. She chose me to open up to; it was meant to be.

I knew that sleeping would not be readily available once I checked into the room and was faced with the time to close my eyes. The night was going to drag, for sure.

While our home life had slowly returned to a calmer place, this was a familiar disruption.

From a processing standpoint, I wondered how upset Aryn was about this sudden turn of events and what this impact would mean to him. Still, considering Kaden's previous medical history, Aryn always knew his brother to have been very ill in some way or another. I hoped this hospital stay, in his eyes, was not any different than those others.

He'd had a difficult time with the instability over the last couple of years but seemed to finally settle in with some structure by having both parents under one roof for a sustained amount of weeks.

Now, here we were, pulling the rug out from under him. Tonight, we were both away again.

Having a medically fragile brother is a tremendous burden for a seven-year-old child. Having already experienced so much with Kaden, we were piling more on out of the blue. None of it was right, fair, or offered any justification.

A child his age should only be thinking about a particular snack being placed in a lunch sack, what cartoons to watch after school, or which neighborhood friend to see after coming home. Instead, for him to be concerned about the medical health of his sibling yet again was borderline criminal.

There we were, two hours away from him again. His brother struggled mightily, and the family unit he knew briefly was once again unpredictable in every sense. Aryn was losing as much as we were through it all.

In the morning, as she had done so many times to help us, Grammy would see him off to school and assure him everything would turn out fine. It worked for the previous two years, and we counted on it to do so again.

The little white lie needed to continue.

It was all we had.

HEADLINE

FRIDAY, MAY 23, 2008

Hurtful images from our past can instantly tear us down and stomp us deep into the packed soil, cowering for blessed relief from their internal image trappings. This day in May was one of the hardest I have ever known. It will never offer me relief, nor is it expected to do so.

What happened is what I concluded to be the beginning of the end for me in countless ways. After this, the person known as "Aric with an A" no longer existed on this planet. I didn't know it then, but I do now.

After a relatively slow start to the morning, some inconsequential results began to trickle in slowly. The first information presented was that Kaden had developed a heart murmur. This made sense; three days earlier, our doctor back home had mentioned that his heart was performing erratically.

While essential, the information was hardly a revelation of his current condition; at least, it was something. We anxiously looked forward to finally discovering more so we could begin immediate treatment and get on with our lives.

Blindly, I still had some crazy notion that, since the holiday weekend was now upon us, we would still make it to Maine and salvage some part of the planned family event back at the cottage. Since they had been running tests for three days, we assumed a definitive diagnosis would soon be forthcoming.

His world once again was being turned upside down by the events that had transpired over the previous three days. I elected to travel home to see Aryn and surprise him by spending some much-needed father-and-son time. Being with him might help minimize disruptions to his daily life.

After grabbing my extra-large cup, I kissed K, who was watching an Elmo video calmly. His green binkie was firmly in place, and a belly now the size of Texas protruded from under the blanket.

Quite truthfully, he cared less about my leaving and more about how I was distracting him from his movie.

At least he wasn't in pain, so all was fine with me.

I loaded the car and left for home at about two p.m. that afternoon. Stacey was to call me if any additional information became available.

One thing I knew for sure by heading home was how happy Aryn would be to see part of his family together again. After this hellish week, we would be half-balanced again in the Morrison home, which was a step in the right direction for both of us. To cap it off, the Celtics were playing game three in the playoff series against Detroit. My plan for later was to watch the game while relaxing with a cold beer.

Around three o'clock, my wife had just returned from taking one of those needed snack breaks, consisting of a warm cup of tea and a Nestle 100-grand bar. She returned to Kaden's room to suddenly see a host of medical professionals deliberately awaiting her return.

They had more news. This time, there were answers.

Stacey was quickly escorted into a conference room directly next door to where our tender, Dora-the-Explorer-watching, patient, little angel-boy was.

Unaware of anything else happening around him but his videos, Kaden sat passively in his hospital bed. His momma received definitive information about what was happening inside his fragile, two-year-old body.

A diagnosis no parent should ever have to process.

Shortly after that, I was utterly unaware that she was frantically trying to reach me repeatedly on the phone. Stacey was trembling beside Kaden now, trying to process what was said to her.

While doing everything possible to hear my voice and share the information, it didn't happen. As luck would have it, that third Friday in May, I was driving through an area of New Hampshire without towers.

It's hard to believe we had the technology to keep a child alive who was born a mere twenty ounces, but we could not figure out how to ensure that cell coverage might exist without any voids.

With her phone in hand, Stacey again frantically dialed my number to no avail. I drove along Interstate 89 South while listening to some of my favorite music without knowing what was happening.

My phone never rang.

By Kaden's side, she gave up after the fourth attempt and cried alone.

I can only liken the rapidly unfolding events of the afternoon to one at some old metropolitan newspaper plant. Someone was working frantically to get the latest scoop to print with the intensity of meeting a deadline.

Rush, rush, rush.

In my head, it must have played out something like this:

"Just in, hot off the presses.

Kaden Harding Morrison is in trouble.

Miracle Baby was just diagnosed.

This twenty-four-month-old toddler faces another battle.

His father cannot be reached for comment.

Extra, extra, read all about it."

Paper, mister?

What we initially thought was a casual visit to the doctor in Peterborough only two days before evolved quickly. A third-day nightmare diagnosis was now cast upon my wife without my awareness of it.

The garbage I dealt with at home while growing up, anxieties, depression, abuse, loss, and inner struggles were about to become instantly inconsequential by comparison.

Like college athletes who play ball, they do so in preparation for making it to the major leagues one day. All my other adversities had just been a warm-up to this one, too.

Without a doubt, we were on the verge of next-level madness.

WORD

Today, we were being escorted without advance notice to the most dangerous place ever known to humankind, ill-prepared and forced entirely against our will. We were the chosen ones standing at the threshold of hell, figuratively knocking in unison to allow us in.

Ironically, we had now become a statistic.

No members of our family would be granted immunity from our next battle. This one possessed the force to rip us apart, leaving nothing behind but sorrow and emptiness.

Earlier that day, a few select people had the unfortunate task of sitting with the mother of a unique, extraordinary, two-year-old baby. They explained that her precious child was being ravaged beyond repair from the inside.

For the previous twenty-four months of his life, Kaden had taken full advantage of every opportunity to command a silently loud voice in expressing his will to survive via his incredible resilience.

This time, to make another case on his behalf, he was still supposed to remain here for his predestined purpose.

As it turned out, our preciously unique baby, who had not yet been able to walk, crawl, or even roll over, was, at this point in his short life, being summoned to somehow defeat a force so powerful it would even cause the likes of a superhero to pause and look away with grave concern.

Our son had already been at war with an enemy all alone. The devastation that had been done to him was significant and definitive. His daddy, mommy, and big brother hadn't realized it was happening.

To some extent, maybe this made hearing the news even more painful.

Aryn's baby brother with crooked front teeth, a scar-riddled body, disabled, saggy skin, a twisted esophagus, feeding tube fed, purity smiling, one leg longer than the other, hearing impaired, heart repaired, frail, green-binkie-sucking, non-verbal, hand flapping, head twitching, Elmo-watching, quiet laughing, perfect little gift, and two-year-old fighter, was already facing evil in its most malefic form. He had been doing so for weeks.

Kaden, who had never spoken a word (let alone babble), his vocal cords thoroughly paralyzed from the intubation, attempted to silently scream aloud at the top of his prematurely and still-forming lungs.

"My life needs to be saved!"

I feared this, like no other scenario, when it came to my children's health.

Now, it was upon me.

This one, by far, had the making to become our most significant challenge. The most indescribably wrenching circumstance in our long and bumpy story as a family was now set in motion as real as the night, and we never saw it coming.

Our one-pound, four-ounce, barely two-year-old, micro preemie, oxygen-tank-dependent, nasal-cannula-wearing fighter was now being overtaken inside by cancer.

Dear God.

POSTGAME

* * *

STARE

My head instantly became the unwilling victim of a hundred-thousand-million thoughts occupying space that Friday evening.

None of them were of any comfort to me.

The clock probably read close to eleven p.m., but then again, I was operating within a blurred timeline. The hours were minutes, and the minutes became hours. Almost as if the hands of time were playing tricks with my psyche.

I was sober-drunk and high, without any actual intake. I'm sure the concept of consciousness hadn't mattered anyway.

Nothing did.

I was unsure who I was.

There alone in the dark, the black-robed master of hopelessness whispered his newest succession of horrid phrases in my ears each time I attempted to shake my head clear of them.

He was back.

Out-of-body became welcome; my fiction became my reality.

My head was a tunnel of turmoil spinning around; colors melted into darkness while my mind turned gray.

The screaming whispers from my adversity past were trying to break my eardrums out of jealousy, all still trying to remain relevant. Based upon this sudden turn of events, they knew they were at risk of becoming obsolete without possessing the same pain-causing stronghold they once held upon me.

I was on the verge of realizing a new level of mind-soak. Just like that, everything was becoming distorted.

Any sense of typical had now passed quickly. Six letters had taken that possibility away from me, and in forever time, the hours passed. They came and went freely without making a sound on any clock.

My solemn reflection upon the events that had transpired also provided a dark backdrop, creating a definitive barrier to closed eyes. Because the critical rush of events had occurred so randomly, attempting to make sense of the day had proved unachievable.

On this night, I was barely breathing, suddenly put into a blank, airless place without any choice in my presence. I am convinced it never wanted me to be there in the first place.

I existed, staring into space somewhere within the universe, merely laying there, contorted, rejecting oxygen in another shadow-filled, strobe-lit, spinning room.

The struggle was like nothing imaginable.

Deep within my chest, a confused heart had stopped beating. My physical body wasn't needed, as I wasn't alive anymore. It was as though I was floating and drowning at the same time.

I didn't belong anywhere, possessing no real purpose or value to anyone but only to stare at the ceiling like a cooling corpse waiting for a final ride.

Was it day or night, black or white?

Was I in a natural or some surreal, altered state?

Only the physical shell of a human presence remained; my soul had abandoned me, trying dutifully to figure out its new course.

Music by The Cure haunted softly in the background through my laptop continually, filling the floaty spaces of time quite appropriately.

It wouldn't have mattered if it had played one song or fifty. None were ever heard or even meant to be. It was loud and soft, electric and acoustic at the same time.

The laughing chuckle of evil constantly beat within my skull as I was on the verge of dizzy-spinning out of control in a cataclysmic and destructive way. After today, logical reasoning wouldn't be familiar ever again.

"Dance for me, Aric, dance."

UNTITLED

I *L*ove you moRe than I ever said.

AFTERWORD

Ironically, our wedding song, "To Make You Feel My Love," sung by Garth Brooks, came on while I began writing this. Is it some sign, a gentle reminder of what was, or just a coincidence?

I always try to connect various happenstances by searching for some deep-seated reason why they occur. Most of the time, this results in me overstretching the truth. Funny, if I pour a glass of wine and do so, it becomes so much easier!

This book required me to expose where my mind was during this alarming phase of my life. I know the next one will be even more difficult because the downward cascade for me was ongoing. Between pursuing professional goals and providing for my family, my home existence was drifting further away from being a healthy environment.

It might have gotten worse, but I wouldn't allow it.

I seek no sympathy in what I do, only to share and, hopefully, via my words, inspire others to keep moving forward through the rainiest of times as I did. When you have a child born shorter than a pretzel rod, it messes with you.

My coffee is still warm, and the third book coming up needs minor attention. Hopefully, I can come out on the other side of that one with much of the same beginnings to seek closure. I am not fearful of going back there; this is the deal with myself that I made when this all began.

We travel through the highs and lows of life. With each day, there is as much potential for frowns as there are smiles. It all depends on how you choose to proceed.

ACKNOWLEDGMENTS

Sometimes, all it takes is a smile, a talk, a look, or simply a listening ear. I love you all for having a meaningful role in my story.

Rick L, Mark H, June U, Eva T, Stacey A, Missy L, Lisa R, Robert S, Jeff A, Cliffy, Reuban, Lisa C, Heidi R, Chris C, Ken F, Kate C, Jim B, Steve A, Car driver to AC, Troup P, Kamau B, TJ M, Dr. Barb, Kim, Dave I, Mario A, Denys M, Tom D, Rich G, Kurt K, Gary M, John M, Eric, Charles S, Gary W, Nick W, Tim D, Molly D, Lydia S, Lisa L, Ed T, Gary, Joe N, John M, Ethan F, Evelyn D, Sandy S, Borden W, Loretta C, Ames, Tom G, Tom D.

And last but certainly not least, my heartfelt appreciation must also go to the mysterious Olivia Jane.

Wherever you are.

ABOUT THE AUTHOR

Aric H. Morrison is a seasoned business executive, boasting over thirty years of experience in various corporate settings. His passion for leadership and people development has been a driving force throughout his career, and he now leverages his wealth of life experiences to assist others in navigating their most challenging professional moments.

Mr. Morrison is a multifaceted professional who excels as an Inspirational Speaker, an Award-Winning Author, an International Writer, and a Multimedia Personality. He is the visionary behind Adversity Rockstar LLC, a platform where he harnesses his creative talents to inspire, motivate, and transform lives through stage speaking, writing, blogs, books, and frequent co-host radio appearances.

To date, he has been seen on TV in over one hundred thirty countries, his blogs are read in over twenty-five, and his books are enjoyed everywhere. While this series has taken its toll, Aric still presents himself daily with a smile.

His dedication to audiences and fans drives him to keep giving back, as he knows he is making a difference in their lives.

Aric is an inspiration, and I am proud to know him.

— KAREN MARONEY, A LIFELONG FRIEND

POSTSCRIPT

There were days when writing this second book took on an entirely new emotional direction for me. Reliving these details is utterly traumatizing in and of itself. However, I continued creating this book with each of you in mind.

If not for sharing and inspiring, why bother?

My belief in describing in sometimes graphic detail exactly what was taking place in real-time for my family and me was fundamental to retelling those moments. How else does one explain the physical nature of a child born just over one pound?

In many respects, our child was almost inhuman to have existed so small. To this day, I still find it incredible to look back upon those early days of his birth.

I hope you can appreciate the design and flow of this series by now. Every chapter title and placement is methodically planned throughout every book in this series. The storytelling is always at risk of compromise unless the author remains true to his vision.

One of the more challenging aspects of writing over one million words is to be confident in the selection process by word, phrase, and sentence. It is an absolute bitch to be so meticulous, but when it is your own life story, perfection is demanded every morning when I look in the mirror to hold myself accountable.

Until the end of this, a creative build is going on in how I shared with you the rushing cadence of constant pushback against our sanity and form of peace within. This is how it was.

When you need to balance the entire family amidst the untimely pressures of constant medical adversities, there is a slow drain that erodes your soul. In this second section, I realized it was happening to me.

I am very proud to have written this book's last chapter in the way it ultimately came out. It wasn't easy to convey exactly what was going on in my racing mind, but I feel this one captured it as close to reality as possible.

I will never forget the night of May 23, 2006. In truth, our family could never return to where we were just one week prior.

This is where I also offer my readers a few cursory words of caution. This second book was deliberately designed in flow to allow you to breathe a bit through most of it until the bottom begins to fall out toward the end.

Know that book number three, *A Declaration of Time*, brings forth a relentlessly moving rush of events. I won't tell you that this next one will play a little on your emotional side.

I will guarantee it.

For now, breathe relief and kiss your children. Celebrate your good fortune, as so many others cannot do so anymore. Cancer is terrible. In a child, it is worse than anything else imaginable.

Bless you for taking this ride back in time with me. And thanks for caring enough to do so.

FINAL

As we conclude the second installment in *The Stealing Home Series*, I sincerely hope you found it to match your expectations, at the very least. If my job was done correctly, it might even have exceeded them.

I am always most grateful and humbled to know how you feel about my literary works. Feel free to drop me an email and let me know. I reply to all messages. My material is too personal. I would never allow someone on my Rockstar Team to represent me in a reply. Know this.

I take my writing, editing, composing, story-telling, design, contemplation, flow, and theming seriously. Anyone who knows me personally will attest that when my name appears, there is always a sense of pride attached to it.

For now, my time here is done. The next book in the series awaits my undivided attention. You can be sure the third one will move your heart as well. It will sneak up on you and leave you grabbing the tissue box.

Thank you once again for the privilege of your time to allow me to share these elements of my life story with you.

Until the next one

Cheers. . . A

ALSO BY ARIC H. MORRISON

HEAVENLY PEACE

CHASING RAINDROPS

A DECLARATION OF TIME

ON IMAGINARY WINGS

BLUE SKYE WHISPERS

LIFETIME WHISPERS

MELANCHOLY WHISPERS

ADVERSITY ROCKSTAR

POSITIVELY SPEAKING

POSITIVELY REFLECTING

POSITIVELY SHARING

More Soon!

www.ingramcontent.com/pod-product-compliance
Lightning Source LLC
Chambersburg PA
CBHW071718120626
46550CB00001B/287